Classical Persian Music

Ella Zonis Classical Persian Music

An Introduction

1973 Harvard University Press, Cambridge, Massachusetts

Publication of this book has been aided by a grant

from the Andrew W. Mellon Foundation.

For Nadia and Leah

Preface

Western interest in the music of Asia is hardly a recent phenom-enon. Indeed, as early as 1767 in his famous *Dictionnaire de musique*, Jean Jacques Rousseau published melodies from Persia and China. During the following century specialized area studies appeared, gradually increasing in quantity and in scientific accuracy. Today, largely under the impetus of ethnomusicology, Asian music has become a subject of study in numerous Western universities. But no longer is this music solely the province of scholars: con-certs and recordings of Asian artists reach large audiences and thereby have influenced the style of many jazz and pop musicians.

As the current enthusiam for Eastern music continues to grow, the music of Persia provides a fresh field of study. For while Indian music is presently the subject of intensive research and Arabian music was focused upon earlier in the century, the art music of Iran has not yet received the thorough analysis accorded that of her neighbors. Investigating this music thus presents the double challenge of exploring a new musical system and of understanding it in terms of the artistic and literary achievements that have long been recognized by the West.

In addition to its intrinsic interest, however, contemporary Persian music merits attention for its possible relationship with the music of ancient Greece. It is not unlikely that both Persian and ancient Greek music had a common source in the musics of Sumeria and the ancient cultures of Asia Minor. And a strong possibility exists that a more direct musical interchange occurred during the long political and cultural contact between Persia and Greece that lasted from the fifth century B.C. into the first three centuries of the Christian Era. Through the influence of Islam, especially Shiʿa Islam, Persia experienced a long musical quiescence which effectively preserved the original form of her art music until the present century. The postulated relationship between Persian music and ancient Greek music thus invites the conjecture that a study of contemporary Persian music will yield further insights into a music now inaccessible.

This study aims to fill a hiatus in the literature of two disciplines. In the field of musicology, little has yet been published on Iran; in Iranological literature, there has been a dearth of publications concerning music. But, since what is basic to members of one field is often unknown to those of the other, writing for two groups as different as musicologists and Orientalists is like steering between Scylla and Charybdis. Indeed, a certain frustration on the part of the reader may be unavoidable, due to either a surfeit or a lack of explanatory material. My policy in the following chapters is to assume a basic knowledge of music terminology but to include background material for the history and culture of Iran.

To the many Iranians who so kindly assisted me during my two years in Persia I here express my warmest appreciation. Mehdi Barkechli generously supplied me with his articles on Persian music and helped me interpret them. Mohammad Heydari and Hossein Malek taught me to play the santur, and Khatereh Parvaneh instructed me in the singing of avaz. Others whose aid and advice are gratefully acknowledged are Manucher Afzal, Amin Banani, H. Dehlavi, Ahmad Ebadi, Ehsan Erfanifar, Mehdi Forough, Zavin Hacobian, Parviz Natal Khanlari, Ibrahim Mansuri, Hossein Nasr, Hushang Partovi, Faramarz Payvar, Dariouche Safvate, Ali Naqi Vaziri, Hushang Zarif, and Mehrdad Pahlbod, who supplied me with one of the first published copies of *La musique traditionelle de l'Iran* and, as Minister of Culture, gave official permission for many parts of my research.

In America this study was aided by Richard Frye. His reading of the introduction and chapter 1 and advice on transliteration are gratefully acknowledged. Hormoz Farhat charted the general direction of my study by suggesting that I learn to play a Persian instrument and by supplying me with names of musicians to contact in Iran, and also made many valuable corrections in the manuscript. I am also indebted to Caldwell Titcomb, Paul Brainard, Bruno Nettl, and William P. Malm, whose many suggestions helped to correct and refine the text. My Japanese colleague in Iran, Gen'ichi Tsuge, participated in many aspects of this project. Knowledgeable friends who read sections of the text and offered musicological criticism are Evelyn Lakoff, Rosamond Brenner, and Ellen Rosand. And, for help with practical details I thank Dorothy Obluda, Paul Obluda, Theodore Wertime, Barbara Spring, Clara Zonis, Lena Zion, and Ann Grant.

The greatest part of the library research for this study was done in Tehran at the home of Mujtaba Minovi, whose collection of works on Persia numbers in the hundred thousand. Besides giving me free rein in his library for many months, Professor Minovi also aided by study of ʿaruz and frequently made suggestions for my reading, often finding rare pamphlets in his enormous files. I should also like to express my gratitude to the authorities of the following libraries for permitting me to use their facilities: the Eda Kuhn Loeb Music Library at Harvard University, the Farmanfarmayan Library at Tehran University, the libraries of the Senate and *Majles* of the Government of Iran, the library of the British Institute of Persian Studies, and the Library of the British Council in Tehran. And to Ali Sheik-ol Islam, who obtained a copy of Hedayat's *Madjmaʿ al Advar* for me, to Lut-follah Payan, who supplied his publications, and to A. Jahan Dari, who rediscovered and led me to the *Bahjat al Ruhʿ*, I here express my thanks. To the Ministry of Art and Culture of the Government of Iran, thank you for the use of *MTI* and three photographs. And to the Victoria and Albert Museum and the British Museum, thank you for the photographs.

My closest friend and teacher in Persia was Ruhollah Khaleqi. During the last years of his life, in spite of painful illness, he gave his time freely to help me understand Persian music. Knowing this great man so enriched my feelings for Iran that I have tried to express my gratitude by fulfilling his often-stated wish to make traditional Persian music known in the West.

The original idea of studying Persian music was not my own.

It was discretely suggested to me in 1962 by my former husband, who scattered bibliographical file cards on Persian music among the notes of my current projects. When I discovered these, my curiosity was whetted and the research begun. Not only did he initiate, finance, and constantly encourage this study, but he also spent countless hours on its manifold technical problems. These ranged from obtaining equipment and recording performances in Iran, to teaching me to read Persian, and to reading the entire manuscript of this book at four stages of its preparation. For his patience and wisdom I am most grateful.

The research for this book was done in 1963–1965, when I was in Tehran. Since then I have kept it up to date by reading and by talking to both Persians here and Americans who have been there. The book is, like classical Persian music, incomplete.

Contents

LIST OF ILLUSTRATIONS

Note on the Transliteration of Persian Words

A simplified version of the conventional Arabic transliteration system has been used in the text, whereby no distinction is made for long and short vowels, and individual characters appear as follows:

ب	b	د	d	ص	s	ک	k	ا	a
پ	p	ذ	z	ض	z	گ	g	و	u
ت	t	ر	r	ط	t	ل	l	ی	i or y
ث	s	ز	z	ظ	z	م	m		
ج	j	ژ	zh	ع	'	ن	n		
چ	ch	س	s	غ	gh	ه	h		
ح	h	ش	sh	ف	f	و	v		
خ	kh			ق	q	ی	y		

Occasionally, a person's name will not be spelled in accordance with this system. If so, it will be his own spelling of his name (for example, Dariouche Safvate), the spelling used in important books, or, in the case of historical figures, the way it is spelled in common usage. In quotations from another author, his system will be preserved. Two systems are used for plurals. The most usual Persian plural form is the suffix "-ha," as in "The dastgah-ha are melody types." But when preceded by a numeral, the noun is left in the singular: "The twelve dastgah are melody types." One special Persian construction which has been observed in the transliteration is the *ezafeh*: A word bearing the suffix "-e" or "-ye" is modified in the word following, as in "Musiqi-ye Iran," Iranian music.

Symbols used in Musical Expressions

∨   left-hand stroke for santur; up stroke for tar

∧   right-hand stroke for santur; down stroke for tar

४ or –   grace note, one note above (half or whole step, depending upon the context)

3   grace note two notes above

9, 8   for santur, indicates that the top notes E or F are to be used rather than the bottom, that is, strings 9 or 8

Classical Persian Music

Abbreviations

DAS	Abol Hassan Saba, *Durey-e Aval-e Santur*, 2d ed. (Tehran, 1958)
DAV	Abol Hassan Saba, *Durey-e Aval-e Violin*, 4th ed. (Tehran, 1960)
DDS	Abol Hassan Saba, *Durey-e Dovom-e Santur* (Tehran, 1956)
DDV	Abol Hassan Saba, *Durey-e Dovom-e Violin*, 3d ed. (Tehran, 1959)
DSS	Abol Hassan Saba, *Dure-e Sevoym-e Santur*, 2d ed. (Tehran, 1958)
DT	Lutfollah M. Payan, *Davazdah Tasnif az Davazdah Avaz* (Tehran, 1960)
JIFMC	*Journal of the International Folk Music Council*
JRAS	*Journal of the Royal Asiatic Society*
LavE	Albert Lavignac and Lionel de la Laurencie, *Encyclopédie de la musique*, pt. I, vol. V (Paris, 1922)
MA	Rudolph d'Erlanger, *La Musique arabe*, 6 vols. (Paris, 1930–1959)
MN	Ali Naqi Vaziri, *Musiqi-ye Nazari* (Tehran, 1934)
MTI	Mehdi Barkechli and Mussa Maᶜruffi, *La Musique traditionelle de l'Iran* (Tehran, 1963)
NM	Ruhollah Khaleqi, *Nazari be Musiqi*, II (Tehran, 1938)
SMI	Ruhollah Khaleqi, *Sargozasht-e Musiqi-ye Iran*, I (Tehran, 1954)

Introduction The Present State of Music in Iran

The spirit of Persia has nearly vanished from modern Iran. Although its monuments are abundant, from the celebrated ruins of Persepolis to the splendors of Esfahan, evidence of a continuation of the culture that produced these monuments—a living evidence of what is uniquely Persian—is rare amid the predominantly Western culture emanating from Tehran. In Iran today, especially in the tumult of the capital, it takes a special wrench of the mind to remember that this is one of the world's oldest civilizations, one that produced truly great art and literature and one that has contributed to the spiritual enrichment of mankind for well over fifty centuries.[1]

Although traditional Persian culture is but dimly apparent in modern Iranian life, it is carefully preserved in centers of scholarship all over the world: in museums, where the numerous art objects and the latest archaeological discoveries from Iran are catalogued and interpreted; in institutes for Persian studies, which support and publish new research; and especially in universities, where the number of departments teaching Persian language and culture has increased markedly during the past decade. The illustrious past of Iran is well appreciated. The present cannot in any measure compare with it.

Considering its exceptional record of cultural vitality and artistic activity through so many centuries, however, Iran might

---

1. Illustrating this long history is an exhibit shown recently in the United States and Europe entitled "Seven Thousand Years of Iranian Art." The catalog by the same title is Smithsonian Institute Publication No. 4535 (Washington, D.C., 1964).

be expected to undergo another renaissance. Meanwhile, like other Asian countries, the nation focuses on modernization. Mohammed Reza Shah Pahlavi, the present king, is continuing the work of his father, Reza Shah, who forced the early stages of Iran's modernization in much the same way that Kamal Ataturk effected the development of Turkey. Basically, modernization has become synonymous with westernization, for Western culture inevitably accompanies Western technology. In this complex process, the indigenous culture is likely to be rejected: not only are traditional methods of farming, transportation, production, and communication cast off, but also the traditional social institutions and the art forms they supported. No longer in keeping with the pace and style of modern Iran, traditional art forms are being neglected in favor of Western art forms or adaptations of native art that are acceptable to newly westernized tastes.

Especially sensitive to social conditions, art music quickly reflects the new aesthetic values accompanying modernization. Thus, in the last fifty years, the most intensive period of westernization in Iran, Persian music has changed significantly after a quiescence of more than ten centuries. Previously, art music in Persia was highly refined, intimate, and subtle. Few Iranians today appreciate this delicate music. A lighter, more rhythmic style has developed to fit the tastes of a growing, Western-oriented middle class, and Western music, both classical and popular, is played throughout Iran to an extent that it threatens to overshadow much traditional Persian music.

Indeed, on first view, Iran's musical scene appears to be dominated by Western music, especially in Tehran, the cultural center of the country. The Tehran Philharmonic Society presents a full concert season of Western classical music featuring the Tehran Symphony Orchestra and many native and foreign soloists and chamber ensembles. There is a classical ballet company in Tehran whose British ballet master is sent by the Royal Ballet for two-year periods; there are even performances of Western operas. The Conservatory of Music, the Ballet School, and scores of Iranian and European music teachers are steadily increasing the supply of performers of Western music. Finally, radio and television broadcast a high proportion of Western-style music, reaching the largest audience of all.

Despite the spread of Western and Western-style music in Iran, a considerable amount of traditional Persian music still exists. Its continuance is due mainly to the notable vitality of Persian culture, with support from the government of Iran, which nurtures traditional music as part of its attempt to preserve indigenous Iranian art.[2] The traditional musics performed today can be grouped into five types. Folk music can be heard among the tribes and peasants. Religious music may be defined as the music of the mosque and of religious festivals. Popular Iranian music is the type of native music most often broadcast on radio and television and played in cafés. Ceremonial musics native to Persia are performed in the zur khaneh (house of strength) and naghareh khaneh (kettledrum house, or the Persian tower music). And, there is traditional classical music, which in its most authentic form is played in private homes and in the meeting places of certain Dervish orders. These five types of Persian music are not always distinct in practice. In addition, they contain many common features and cross influences. As background to a more detailed examination of the classical music, I will consider all five forms briefly.

FOLK MUSIC

The majority of Iran's twenty-two million inhabitants live outside the large cities in scattered towns and villages. A large number of tribes, many still nomadic, are an important part of this population. These rural peoples are scattered over an extensive area of extremely inhospitable terrain where, until recently, communications were poorly developed or nonexistent. Thus, most of these groups have remained relatively isolated from each other and from the culture of the cities. Furthermore, the peasants and tribesmen of Iran represent many different ethnic

---

2. The Ministry of Art and Culture sponsors a separate conservatory of national music, several orchestras of native instruments, and a group of musicologists who collect and publish examples of Persian music.

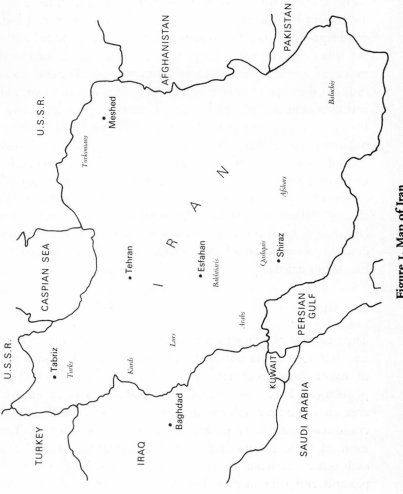

Figure 1. Map of Iran

Semiprofessional folk musicians of the Ministry of Art and Culture playing the surna, naghareh, and daff.

backgrounds, places of origin, and languages. In fact, nearly half the population speaks languages other than Persian.[3] Many of these language groups form distinct sub-cultures, each having its own folk music.

In the northwest section of Iran is a large Turkic-speaking population whose folksongs and dances are similar in style to their counterparts in the Soviet Union. Sizeable groups of Assyrians and Armenians with their own languages and music inhabit the urban areas of this section. Moving south, there are Kurdish- and Luri-speaking tribes. Arabs inhabit the southwest section of Iran from the border of Iraq along the Persian gulf towards Pakistan.

The central section of the country, which extends from the Caspian Sea south to the Persian Gulf, contains the three major cities of Iran: Tehran, Esfahan, and Shiraz. Outside the cities,

3. *Iran Almanac 1963* (Tehran, 1963), p. 481.

many local dialects are spoken by the rural population. The most important linguistic groups in this central section are the Gilaki in the north, and the Bakhtiari and Qashqai in the south.

Inhabiting the northeast province of Gorgan are the Turkomans, of Central Asian origin, with a musical culture similar to that of Soviet Turkmenistan. And in the southeast are the Baluchi tribes with their own language.

Hence, within the borders of Iran are many distinct and important folk cultures offering a rich field of study for the ethnomusicologist. The Iranian government itself has undertaken some of the musicological field work necessary to investigate this folk material. More than a decade ago, research teams were despatched to the major linguistic areas, where they gathered a large collection of tape recordings with accompanying photographic, biographical and geographical data. This is now housed in the Ministry of Culture, and, although some of this material has been transcribed and published, the bulk of this rich collection remains untouched.[4]

In the area of folk dancing, the government encourages provincial musicians and dancers, frequently offering them professional training in Tehran. The result appears to be a professionalization of what was formerly a completely folk art. Groups of semiprofessional dancers and instrumentalists now give remarkably polished performances in Tehran and, fortified by members of the National Ballet Company, have also been sent abroad. Many Iranian folk dances have been adapted for performance by the professional ballet in Tehran.

RELIGIOUS MUSIC

A consideration of religion is especially important when discussing Persian music. For, aside from the folk and popular music, most Persian music is essentially religious in spirit. Persian art music

---

4. Publications of Persian folk music are those of Mobassheri, Payan, Sheybani, and Mahmudi (see bibliography). The number of musicological studies of Iranian folk music by foreigners is small. For the German expedition to Kurdistan, see Dieter Christensen, "Brautlieder der Hakkari-Kurden," *Jahrbuch für musikalische Volks- und Völkerkunde* I (1963), 11–47, and *Kurdish Folk Music from Western Iran*, recorded by Dieter and Nerthus Christensen, Ethnic Folkways Library FE 4103.

is quiet and very serious, frequently inspiring the profound emotions that one normally associates with Western church music. The texts for traditional art music are most often the mystic poems of Rumi (thirteenth century) and Hafez (fourteenth century) which express basically religious sentiments in such symbols as love and wine. But, curiously enough, even though so much of Persian music is religious, the official religion of Iran is antipathetic to music. This irony forms one of the recurring themes of the present study, for the Persian attitude toward music, which was shaped by Islam, has had a critical effect on the music itself for an extraordinarily long time.

Like several other religions that had their beginnings in the Middle East, Islam took a cautious view of music during its first centuries, because music had come to be associated with revelry and licentious conduct. But whereas Christianity, for example, gradually relaxed its disapproval and ultimately became an invaluable patron of music, Islam did not. Indeed, the Islamic disapprobation of music grew even stronger as the religion became firmly established. Only music for holy wars, for celebrations of a sacramental nature, and for the chanting of the Koran was officially sanctioned.[5] Although during certain periods when religious restrictions were relaxed, musical activities flourished in the courts of the Caliphs, the predominant attitude in Islamic culture was antimusical. This was reinforced during the sixteenth and seventeenth centuries when Shiᶜa Islam, in contrast to orthodox Sunni Islam, was declared the state religion and used as a tool for the creation of Iranian nationalism.[6] Religious

5. M. L. Roychoudhury, "Music in Islam," *Journal of the Royal Asiatic Society* 23 (1957), 101. See also Amnon Shiloah, "L'Islam et la musique," *Encyclopédie des musiques sacrées*, ed. Jacques Porte (Paris, 1968).

6. Although the Shiᶜa sect of Islam gives allegiance to the Prophet Mohammed, it does not accept the orthodox line of the Prophet's successors but instead recognizes Ali, son-in-law of Mohammed, and Ali's descendants. Stemming from the different interpretation of succession, there have arisen important differences of doctrine and of ceremonial practice. The majority of Moslems are Sunni, but Shiᶜism is the official religion of Persia, and there are sizable numbers of Shiᶜa Moslems in Iraq, India, Pakistan, and Syria. According to G. E. von Grunebaum, "Shiᶜism differs from Sunnism, the so-called orthodox Islam, both in its emotional atmosphere and in its principal intellectual motivations. The religious sensibilities are keener, emotional responses to doctrine more intense, exclusivism and fanaticism closer to the surface than in Sunni Islam." *Muhammadan Festivals* (London, 1958), pp. 85–86.

fervor was then renewed, and once again music was subject to discrimination.

At the same time that music was officially condemned by the Islamic clergy, it was actively championed by a most significant group within Islam, the Sufis. In these mystic orders, which developed outside of the legalistic framework of Islam, music is considered one of the chief means by which man can attain union with God.[7] And because they regard music as bringing the soul to a state of equilibrium and clarity, almost all Sufis, with the exception of a few orders, participate in what are called "sacred concerts."[8] Significantly most of the important Persian musicians of the late medieval and modern periods have been members of Sufi orders. For this reason, many Iranians claim that the serious, mystical character of Persian music is due to the close relationship between music and the mystic orders within Islam. Thus, the subject of religion and music in Persia has broader ramifications than might be expected in another culture. On the one hand, the official religion of Persia condemns music; on the other hand, most Persian music is religious in spirit. For our purposes, however, religious music will be defined as the music of the mosque and of sacred celebrations, and the music used by Sufi musicians will be considered part of the traditional art music.

Little has been written in Western languages describing the cantillation of the Koran in Persia.[9] This may be due to the restrictions against non-Muslims in Shiʿa houses of worship, or to the sensitivity of devout Muslims with regard to music. Another reason may simply be that the attention of musicologists, still concentrated on folk and art music, has not yet been directed to religious music. Examples would not be difficult to obtain, for religious music is now broadcast by microphone to the streets

7. The most important Sufi order from the musical point of view is the Mevlevi sect, founded in Anatolia by Jalal ed-Din Rumi (d. 1273).

8. Cyprian Rice, *The Persian Sufis* (London, 1964), p. 99. For additional reading on music and the Sufi orders, see Helmut Ritter, "Der Reigen der 'Tanzenden Derwische,' " *Zeitschrift für vergleichende Musikwissenschaft* I (1933), ii; M. Mokri, "Le Soufisme et la musique," *Encyclopédie de la musique* (Paris, 1961), pp. 1014–1015.

9. Si Hamza Boubakeur, "Psalmodie iranique," *Encyclopédie des musiques sacrées*, pp. 388–403; Nelly Caron, "La musique Shüte en Iran," ibid., pp. 430–440.

outside the mosque. It is also transmitted by radio on Friday, the weekly holy day, and during such religious periods as Ramazan, the month of daytime fasting. Even some commercial phonograph recordings of cantillation have been produced in Tehran.

One of the most fascinating aspects of Persian religious music, and one said to be indigenous to Iran, is the religious drama or tazieh. These are passion plays given during the lunar month of Moharram to reenact the murder of Hossein, the third Immam, who with his followers are the martyrs of Shi'a Islam. Commemoration of their passion and death is central to this sect.[10] All during the month of Moharram, special black tents are erected in the cities and towns of Iran for the production of tazieh. There are several plays, set in different historical periods, all dealing with the martyrdom of Hossein.[11] Singing or chanting their lines, the actors use traditional melodies, the same found in the dastgah-ha, or melody types, of Persian art music. Each of the play's characters sings in one dastgah, certain dastgah-ha being traditional for the heroes and others for the villains. Many of these passion plays contain instrumental interludes, most typically for the surna (oboe) and the dahal (drum).[12]

On the ninth and tenth days of Moharram there are numerous religious processions where the martyrs of Shi'a Islam are mourned with chanting and recitations. The marchers often flagellate themselves with special chains or beat their chests in rhythm to create the passion of Hossein.[13]

10. Hossein, son of Ali and thus grandson of the Prophet, and his followers were massacred on the tenth of Moharram in 680 while on their way to lead a revolt against the Omayyad Caliph of Damascus. The murders occurred sixty miles southwest of Baghdad on the plain of Kerbala, now the most sacred goal of Shi'a pilgrimages.

11. The anachronism of the settings is one of the notable characteristics of tazieh.

12. A bibliography for tazieh is given in von Grunebaum, *Muhammadan Festivals* p. 101. Additional references are: A. Chodzko, *Théâtre persan* (Paris, 1878); Medjid Rezvani, *Le théâtre et la danse en Iran* (Paris, 1963); Charles Virolleaud, *Le théâtre persan ou le drame de Kerbela* (Paris, 1950). I am also grateful to Peter Chelokowsky for information on tazieh.

13. The Shi'as have added two ideas to the original message of Islam. One is the concept of the Immam, the "bearer of the divine light," who is also the spiritual and political leader of the community. The other is that of " 'the passion' or of vicarious suffering, and it is this that has principally determined the mood of the Shi'a." Von Grunebaum, *Muhammadan Festivals*, pp. 85–86.

POPULAR MUSIC

The music most frequently heard in the cities on radio and television and in cafés and night clubs is Iranian popular music.
Most phonograph recordings made in Iran are also of this type
of music. It reflects numerous foreign influences, not only from
Western, but also from Arabic, Turkish, and Indian musics.

The major form of Iranian popular music is the ballad, or
tasnif, whose source dates back to pre-Islamic times.[14] A recent
flourishing of tasnif composition occurred during the first
decade of the twentieth century, when tasnif-ha were used as
satirical comments during the increased political activity sur-
rounding the creation of the Iranian constitution in 1906. Tasnif-
ha from this period may be considered part of the art music of
Iran, since they were composed in one of the dastgah-ha and
are close to the melodies of that dastgah in their basic structure.
But many tasnif-ha written more recently, especially those of the
last twenty-five years, are generally of a lighter character and
closer to Western popular music. That is, they may be written in
a major or minor mode rather than in one of the more exotic
dastgah-ha; their rhythms may be those of Western dances,
such as the tango; and modern tasnif-ha may be harmonized and
orchestrated. In addition, the melodies are often less florid and
simpler in structure than those of classical music.

This type of native Iranian music has the accouterments of
any popular, commercial music. Tasnif singers are idolized by
the public, and details of their lives, especially the more
scandalous ones, often appear in the newspapers. Hit songs are
printed and sold in the streets along with magazines featuring
articles about the songwriters and singers. Collections of popular
tasnif-ha arranged for guitar, accordion, or piano are frequently
published.

CEREMONIAL MUSIC: MUSIC OF THE NAGHAREH KHANEH AND ZUR
KHANEH

Two very special types of ceremonial music still exist in parts of
Iran. The naghareh khaneh, or Persian tower music, is an extra-

---

14. See pp. 172–179. See also Bruno Nettl, "Persian Popular Music," *Ethnomusicology* 16
(1972), 218–239.

The singer and drummer of the Zur Khaneh at the Jafari Sports Club, Sayed Akbar Sharif Shirazi. Note the electric heater used to prepare the drumhead.

ordinary institution that held a special fascination for European travelers to Iran during the seventeenth, eighteenth, and nineteenth centuries. Writing at the beginning of the last century, George Curzon described "the sonorous and portentous discord which is evoked every evening by the band of brazen-lunged youths to whom I used to listen with a horrified fascination at Tehran ... Every evening at sundown is discoursed from prodigious horns, kettledrums, cornets and fifes, the appalling music which is an inalienable appurtenance of royalty in Persia and is always sounded at sunset from some elevated gallery or tower in any city blessed with a royal or princely governor."[15] Curzon also quotes Chardin, a traveler in Iran two hundred years earlier, who made the comment that this "musik [sic] would never charm a curious ear!"[16]

Unfortunately for curious ears, the naghareh khaneh is rapidly disappearing. In Tehran, only the tower is left, although on rare occasions groups similar to naghareh khaneh play in the city park. Present-day performances of this music which I heard in Meshed were not any more musical than in the time of Curzon. For most of the ten-minute performance, the kettledrums (naghareh) drowned out the woodwinds, leaving only a shrill bleating indefinite pitch and dubious melodic content.

Even more colorful and now featured as one of Tehran's chief tourist attractions is the zur khaneh (house of strength). In mirrored, octagonal rooms attached to sports clubs, traditional Persian ceremonial exercises are performed to the accompaniment of a virtuoso drummer who also chants from the famous epic poem the Shah Nameh.[17]

15. George Curzon, Persia and the Persian Question (London, 1812), pp. 309–310.

16. Ibid., p. 309. The nagareh khaneh was also used by the Moghuls of India, whose courtly culture was chiefly Persian. The instruments and hours of playing are described in detail by the court chronicler of the emperor Akbar (r. 1556–1605), Abul Fazl, in the Ain i Akbari. The sections on music, translated by H. Blockman, are given in S. M. Tagore, ed., Hindu Music from Various Authors (Calcutta, 1875), pp. 211–213. Ruhollah Khaleqi reports that the Safavid emperor Shah Abbas brought nagareh khanch players from India to Iran. SMI, p. 199.

17. A recording of this music has been issued in Paris: Musée de l'Homme, Iran, Musique Persan, Enregistrements de Nöel Ballif, Vogue EXTP 1033 et 1034, vol. 1 et 2: Musique de Zour Khaneh.

CLASSICAL MUSIC

The art music of Persia is primarily a music of the cities. Developed under the patronage of the royal court, classical music was also extensively used by certain Sufi orders. Owing to the religious disapproval of Islam, this music was rarely performed in public and was restricted to the court and private homes. Thus, for thirteen centuries, Persian art music has not been a concert music. Indeed, the character of the most traditional art music clearly reflects its private function. Performed by very small groups or by soloists, it is quiet and meditative. Even the instruments are mainly of delicate timbre. The typical setting for classical Persian music is a home or garden where the musicians are surrounded by a small group of family and friends.

Public performances of Persian classical music began only in the twentieth century. The first large concert, held in a garden on the outskirts of Tehran, was sponsored by a Dervish group, the Okhovat Society. In the late 1920s and the 1930s, several concerts were organized each year by the renowned musician Ali Naqi Vaziri at his conservatory. Additional concerts in the following decades were given by Ruhollah Khaleqi, founder of a society for Persian music. Today concerts of Persian art music in Tehran are often sponsored by foreign cultural organizations, such as the British Council or the United States Information Service. The Ministry of Art and Culture of the Iranian Government also presents a few concerts, but these are usually of folk or popular music.[18] But since the number of concerts of Persian music in Tehran rarely exceeds a half-dozen each year, Persian music cannot yet be considered a public art form.

Since World War II, radio has become an important medium for bringing Persian music to the public. Radio and television may be regarded as a compromise between the traditional setting of the private home and the public performance. Even though the mass media reach a large audience, the listener remains

18. Much of the Persian music sponsored by agencies of the Iranian government and played on radio and television is not the traditional music, but a hybrid form in which Iranian melodies have been harmonized and orchestrated.

in the privacy of his own home, and may partake of the music at his own discretion.

The classical music of Persia is referred to in various ways: musiqi-ye asil (noble music),[19] the music of the radif (the repertory of traditional melodies), or simply dastgah music. It is played either by a solo instrumentalist or, more typically, by an ensemble consisting of singer, instrumentalist, and drummer. When performed by a soloist, Persian art music is monophonic, although chords are used occasionally for decorative purposes, and in some forms there may be a pedal note sounded throughout the piece. Music played by an ensemble is heterophonic—that is, the melody presented by the singer is echoed and varied slightly by the instrumentalist—but again, there is no real harmonic or contrapuntal accompaniment.

Classical Persian music is improvised, the musician being at once performer and composer. Hence, each performance of the same dastgah, even by the same performer, is expected to be different. In performances where the player is before a small group of friends, the improvisation is partially controlled by glances and verbal suggestions between the performer and his audience. Because of this subtle communication the mood of the listeners determines the character and often the form of the player's improvisation.

The repertory of classical Persian music is organized into seven dastgah and five auxiliary dastgah called naghmeh (melody). Each dastgah contains from ten to thirty melodies known as gusheh. These gusheh-ha have been handed down orally for what is claimed to be many centuries; but although according to Persian speculation, some are of genuinely medieval origin, most are more recent. Within the past fifty years, these traditional melodies have been transcribed in Western staff notation, and there now exists a written collection of approximately two hundred fifty gusheh in the twelve dastgah.[20] This repertory of

---

19. I was not aware that this name was meant literally. But one Iranian publication gives the following definition of musiqi-ye asil: "It is considered royal music and is fostered by the Shahs." *Iran Almanac 1963*, p. 486.

20. *MTI*, a collection of many pieces in each gusheh, contains four hundred seventy pieces.

melodies, which forms the basis of classical Persian music, is known as the radif (row). Several transcriptions of the radif have been published, enabling today's student to learn the body of traditional Persian music from printed instruction manuals.

Despite the growing predilection for Western music, a considerable variety of traditional music can still be heard in Iran. Though classical music occupies a relatively small portion of the whole spectrum of traditional music, it is interrelated with the other genres—folk music, religious music, and popular music. Persian art music is religious in spirit and uses religious or semi-religious texts; it has been nurtured and refreshed by Iranian folk music,[21] and in turn, it forms the basis for much of the popular music.

These relationships between art music and the other types of music in Iran will become more apparent in the course of the present study as we examine Persian classical music from a number of complementary vantage points. First is the historical. Knowledge of the country and its history elucidates not only the nature of the people who make and listen to the music, but also the significant historical attitudes toward music that have shaped its development in Iran. An overall view of the history of the music itself will provide a broader perspective for our considera-tion of the present-day art.

A second dimension in this study of Persian art music, the dimension of theory, considers the abstract materials from which Persian music is constructed: the melody type or gusheh, the collection of melody types called the dastgah, the Persian scale and its intervals and the rhythmic modes. Another facet of this study is the melodic material on which improvised performances are based, the radif.

After describing each dastgah in the radif, it is necessary to discover what the performer does to create a composition. If we consider the radif to be information or musical material handed

---

21. Numerous folk tunes have entered the repertory of melodies used for classical music, the radif. These may be easily recognized by their names: for example, in Dashti there are melodies named Gilaki and Daqhestani; in Homayun, one called Bakhtiari. Although these names indicate rural localities or are names of regional tribes, the tunes so called are not always authentic.

down to the musician by tradition, we must next discover how the performer uses this information; in other words, we must study extemporaneous composition or improvisation. This fourth aspect includes ornamentation, rhythm, form, and the use of poetry. Recently musicians have tended to play also from a repertory of nonimprovised, composed music. Its most important forms, the tasnif, pish-daramad (before the daramad, or overture), and reng (dance) will be discussed in relation to contemporary performance practice.

The instruments used to perform Persian music have a long history and are important as predecessors of many European musical instruments. They will be described and their historical background traced. Although some native instruments have been replaced by European ones, others are still widely played. But it is quite likely that those that have remained in use will continue only so long as Persian art music is practiced. In Iran, as all over Asia, the problems of the preservation of traditional music are considerable. These problems and their attempted solutions will be discussed along with an evaluation of the present state of classical music in Persia.

I The Historical Background

One of the most striking characteristics of classical Persian music, especially for the foreign listener, is its pervasive sadness. Iranians are aware of this impression and explain it readily. The Persians, they say, are basically a serious, mystical people, and this sad, quiet music is peculiarly well suited to their philosophy of life and their emotional needs.[1] One seeking the cause of this special national character is reminded of the Iranian countryside—indeed a plausible explanation, since few countries possess such an inhospitable geography. With the exception of a narrow forested belt of land along the Caspian Sea in the north, Iran is composed of desert and mountain. These huge stretches of desert, great vacant spaces broken only by barren mountains, are awesome. The Iranian plateau is often likened to the face of the moon; for, in contrast to Europe and much of Asia to the east, Iran is an empty country, vast and lonely. Once the desolation of this countryside has been experienced, it becomes understandable that the sight of the most insignificant tree or a tiny stream can have a strong effect upon a Persian, and that these should be greatly celebrated in Persian poetry.

It may well be that the character of the land has imposed itself onto the collective character of the Persian people—that they are sad because nature has given them little to enjoy. Persians, however, frequently offer a more compelling explanation of their natural character—their long, tragic history, full of invasions and

---

1. Like Persian music, the religion of Iran, Shiᶜa Islam, is basically sad, with emphasis on mourning periods and martyrdom.

foreign occupations. In the two and one-half millennia since Cyrus the Great (r. 559–530 B.C.), Persia has had only three powerful native dynasties: the Achaemenid (sixth to fourth centuries B.C.), the Sassanian (third to seventh centuries A.D.), and the Safavid (sixteenth to early eighteenth centuries). This lack of strong national rule becomes even more significant with the realization that from the end of the second great native dynasty, A.D. 642, until the present time, a period of 1300 years, only the two centuries under Safavid rule produced an era of Persian greatness. Between these periods of native Persian rule were years of foreign domination and foreign influence that, according to the Persians themselves, have left a scar on the Persian character, a scar that is manifested in the music of today.

The conquest that effected the strongest influence upon Persian music—and indeed upon most aspects of Persian life—was, of course, the Islamic conquest in the seventh century. The great intellectual movements of the ninth and tenth centuries, which resulted in the translation of the Greek philosophers into Arabic and the writing of the great Perso-Arabic treatises on music, left Persian musicians with a concern for the science of music, especially the measurement of intervals. This preoccupation with the mathematical and metaphysical sides of music is evident in the contents of all the theoretical treatises produced in Iran from the tenth century onward and is reflected even today in the Persian attitude that a country's music ought to have a scientific basis to be respectable.[2]

If the coming of Islam gave to Persian music a particular direction, it performed a serious disservice at the same time, for although the Arabs looked with favor on the theory of music, they disapproved of the practice.[3] Thus, the Islamic prohibition

2. Most of these treatises are listed in Henry G. Farmer, *The Sources of Arabian Music*, rev. ed. (Leiden, 1965). To my knowledge, there is presently no extensive bibliography of music treatises in the Persian language.

3. Ibn Kaldun, a well-known Arab historian of the fourteenth century, illustrates the Islamic attitude toward music in his *Muqaddimah*: "[Muslim religious severity] is directed against all activities of leisure and all the things that are of no utility in one's religion or livelihood. Therefore [music] was avoided to some degree. In their [the early Muslims'] opinion only the cadenced recitation of the Qur'an and the humming of poetry which had always been their way and custom, were pleasurable things . . . The craft of singing is the last of the crafts attained in civilization, because it constitutes [the last development toward] luxury with regard to no occupation in particular save that of leisure and gaity." Ibn Kaldun, *Muqaddimah*, trans. Franz Rosenthal, 3 vols. (London, 1958), II, 395–405.

against music eliminated for Persian music what was the most important stimulus to music in the West—the patronage of the church. In the face of opposition from religious leaders, Persian art music was driven underground and kept alive only in the privacy of the royal court or the nobleman's home, out of public view. Even though the effectiveness of the prohibition varied from century to century depending on the relative power of the king and the clergy, the social pressures against the performance of music resulting from this attitude did serve to keep Persian music from extensive technical development over a period of many centuries.

The character of Persian music was also decisively affected by another series of conquests, those of the Turks and the Mongols in the eleventh through the fifteenth centuries. These years are still remembered for the cruelty of the Mongol rulers and the large-scale destruction they wrought in Persia. During this period of turbulence and horror, the Persians, responding through mysticism, wrote much of their greatest poetry. From this time onward, most musicians were members of Sufi orders. Through them Persian mysticism exerted a considerable influence on Persian music, and it is quite likely that the serious character and devotional quality of the music reflect its development by Sufi musicians. Furthermore, mystic poetry still provides the texts for all serious art music.[4]

A major concern in this study of contemporary Persian music is recent Persian history. Here the most important factor, one that continues the pattern of Persian history, is yet another invasion, the cultural invasion of the West. With its predominant quality of secularism, this more peaceful invasion is again changing the Persian attitude toward music, just as the influence of Western music is rapidly changing the music itself.

The history of Persian music was decisively shaped by all these invasions. Not only did foreign occupations influence the theory and practice of the music itself as well as the musical instruments, but they also did much to mold the character and the attitudes of the people who create this music. Because

---

4. From what historians presently know of medieval Persian music, there was virtually no important secular art music. In effect, the music of the Sufis, which was also performed in the royal courts, formed the entire body of Persian art music.

knowledge of a culture's attitudes toward its music is crucial to an understanding of the music itself, the history of Persian music will be preceded by a short review of Persian history.

A SYNOPSIS OF PERSIAN HISTORY

For those unfamiliar with the political history of Iran, a helpful guide is an outline that contrasts the three great national Persian dynasties with the four major foreign occupations. Details may be filled in around these historical landmarks.[5]

Ancient period
    Achaemenid empire[6]   6th to 4th centuries B.C.
    Greek conquest and cultural influence 4th century B.C. to
      during Parthian dynasty   2nd century A.D.
    Sassanian empire   3rd to 7th centuries

Medieval period
    Islamic conquest and cultural influence 7th to 10th centuries
    Turkish and Mongolian conquests   11th to 15th centuries

Renaissance period
    Safavid kingdom   16th to 18th centuries

Modern period
    Western political and cultural   19th and 20th centuries
      influence

The Achaemenid empire at its apogee extended geographically from Egypt eastward to the Indus River in what is now Pakistan, and chronologically from the sixth to the fourth century B.C.

---

5. For general histories of Iran, consult Percy Sykes, *A History of Persia* (London, 1930), and Richard Frye, *Iran* (New York, 1953). See also Frye's outline, pp. 30–31.

6. An important event in Persian history before the Achaemenid period is the coming of the Aryans to the Iranian plateau in the middle of the second millennium B.C. The name Iran comes from Aryan; and Persian, like Hindi and unlike Arabic, is an Indo-European language. This linguistic connection began Iran's relation with the West and is important to her both for what she contributed to Western civilization and for what she gained from it. The most recent period in Persian history, completing the cycle, again refers to the West.

Cyrus the Great, founder of this mighty empire, was succeeded by Cambyses and the brilliant Darius, whose son Xerxes is well known to Western students for his attempted conquests in Greece and his defeat at the battle of Thermopylae. When Alexander the Great conquered the Achaemenid empire in 330 B.C., he sought to combine the two mightiest civilizations of his world, the Greek and the Persian. His early death prevented the joining of these two peoples under one great leader. But although Alexander's empire fell to pieces soon after his death, they were "Hellenic pieces."[7] Greek influence remained strong in Persia for several centuries, for the Seleucids who took over the rule of Persia were Greeks; and even the next dynasty, the Parthians, of Iranian origin, continued the use of Greek language and culture.[8]

The second great native Persian dynasty was the Sassanian, which ruled Iran from the third to the seventh century A.D. Under a long line of able kings, the Sassanians created the Persian empire anew, extending it from Syria well into Central Asia. Just as their predecessors, the Achaemenians, challenged the supremacy of Greece, the great Western power of their day, the Sassanians clashed with the Roman empire and its successor, the Byzantine empire.

Besides being encircled by foreign enemies—the Romans to the west, the Huns in the northeast, and fierce tribes in the north—the Sassanians were plagued by many internal conflicts. While Zoroastrianism was the state religion, there were sizeable Christian minorities in the empire, especially in the province of Armenia. When Rome adopted Christianity, these Iranian Christians were regarded as a fifth column. In addition, other religious movements, for example the Manichaeans, grew powerful and challenged the established order. And finally, the rigid caste system of the Sassanians gave rise to socialist movements

---

7. Frye, *Iran*, p. 40.

8. The Parthians are known to us from accounts by Roman authors. They describe the Roman expeditions against the Parthians led by such notable leaders as Crassus, Mark Anthony, Trajan, and Septimus Severus.

such as the Mazdakites, who posed a serious threat to the royal power.[9]

After four exhausting centuries of wars and of social and religious unrest, this once powerful empire was unable to resist the impact of a new, dynamic civilization. Hence the Arabs, "animated by burning zeal and unlimited self-confidence,"[10] took less than twenty years to complete their conquest of Iran. They remained for almost two centuries, but their religion, alphabet, calendar, and other cultural influences remained for thirteen.

It should be carefully noted that seventh-century Persia became an *Islamic* country, not an *Arabic* one. Within a few centuries, Arabic rule in Persia was supplanted by the rule of native Persian dynasties. In time, Persia made her own language famous in literature and went on to displace other traces of Arabic culture. Islam, however, has remained a crucial part of Persian life to the present day, even though there is a religious difference in addition to the racial and linguistic differences separating Arab and Persian. Islam is the state religion of both groups, but in Iran it is Shiʿa Islam as opposed to the Islam of the Arab countries, which is Sunni.[11] For innumerable reasons, political as well as religious, the Sunni-Shiʿa rift in Islam is as important as the Catholic-Protestant split within Christianity and raises as many, if not more, emotional conflicts.

The Arabic-Islamic civilization, which was to become one of the greatest spiritual and intellectual forces of the Middle Ages, derived much from the older civilizations that it conquered. According to the Persian view, contact with Iran transformed Islam from a local religious movement into an international civilization. One historian even speaks of the "Persian conquest of Islam."[12] Although the first Arab dynasty to rule Persia, the Umayyad caliphate, with its capital in Damascus, was more interested in the western half of the empire and its expansion

9. The basic work for the Sassanian period is Arthur Christensen, *L'Iran sous les Sassanides* (Copenhagen, 1944). See also chapter 6 of Richard Frye's *The Heritage of Persia* (London, 1962).
10. Arthur U. Pope, *A Brief Outline of Persian Art* (New York, 1945), p. 5.
11. See Introduction, note 6.
12. Frye, *Heritage*, p. 249.

into Spain,[13] Persian influence increased with the second caliphate. The Abbasids were Arabs, but they started their military revolt in the northeastern province of Khorrasan in Persia. Now the capital of the empire was much closer to Persia, at Baghdad, and the Abbasids, greatly influenced by legends of the Sassanian empire, attempted to revive the pomp of the Sassanian era. This was the Golden Age of Islam. Baghdad, the capital of an empire that stretched from Spain to Central Asia, was a prominent intellectual center not only for the Near East but also for Europe. The role that this Islamic civilization played in transmitting ancient Greek culture to Europe is well known. During the ninth and tenth centuries, the writings of Greek philosophers were translated into Arabic at Baghdad and used in the great Arab universities in Spain, and were translated into Latin and circulated throughout Europe.

In the second century of Abbasid rule, a series of overlapping independent dynasties arose in Persia, gradually diminishing her loyalty to the Arab caliphate. The most important of these dynasties that ruled over parts of Iran for almost two centuries were three: the Tahirids, with their court at Nishapur in Khorassan (820–873); the Samanids (874–999), whose court in Bukhara is known for its revival of Persian literature and its patronage of the great philosopher Ibn Sina (Avicenna, 980–1037); and the last Persian dynasty before the Turkish invasion, the Buwayhids (932–1055), who came from the Caspian area.

Yet this disjointed renaissance of Persian rule was short-lived. Turks from Central Asia who had been steadily infiltrating the caliphate gained control of Persia in the middle of the eleventh century. Their empire extended from Chinese Turkestan in Central Asia to the Mediterranean and present-day Turkey. Here it is significant that, whereas the latter area, Anatolia, totally absorbed the culture of the Seljuk Turks and today is the center of Turkish culture, Persia maintained her identity and, in fact, culturally subjugated her conquerors.

The next invasion, however, was a major cataclysm for

---

13. The Arabs entered Spain in 711, and only one year later they reached the eastern-most part of their empire, the province of Sind in India.

Iran. Indeed, this period is remembered as the darkest in Persian history. Genghis Khan, who made the first raid on Persia in 1221, and his successors not only sacked cities but destroyed the agricultural systems of entire provinces.[14] The Il-Khans ruled Persia from early in the thirteenth century until late in the fourteenth, when yet another reign of destruction was initiated by Tamerlane, a Central Asian Turk. History credits Tamerlane with two outstanding and somewhat contradictory achievements —his great destruction and his equally great patronage of the arts. Because Persia's relation to Central Asia was particularly strong during the Timurid period, much of the Persian art produced at Tamerlane's capital, Samarkand, displays a Chinese influence.

Finally, after nine centuries of almost constant foreign occupation, a great Persian dynasty arose, recreating Persian civilization just as the Sassanians had done after five centuries of Hellenic domination. The Safavids, who originated in northwestern Iran, in Azerbaijan, were members of the Shiʿa branch of Islam. Declaring Shiʿa Islam to be the state religion of Iran, this dynasty purposely created a religious island between the Sunni countries to the west and to the east. The resulting religious warfare served to establish internal solidarity in Persia, an area that for centuries had been merely a segment of larger empires.[15]

Wars against the Ottoman Turks in the west and the Uzbek Turks in the east occupied most of the sixteenth century. By the time of the most famous Safavid king, Shah Abbas (r. 1587–1628), relative peace was secured, and the reign of this monarch was one of the most prosperous and brilliant in the history of Persia. The country was unified, roads and canals rebuilt, and the magnificent capital at Esfahan constructed. The famous square in this city where Shah Abbas watched his nobles play polo has become, like the figures on the friezes of Persepolis, a favorite subject of Persian iconography. At the height of its glory,

14. In 1258 the sacking of Baghdad by Hulagu Khan, grandson of Ghengis Khan, ended the Abbasid caliphate, which had still been ruling the western part of the empire even though its hold on Iran had been loosened several centuries earlier.

15. The importance of religion during the founding of this dynasty had an important effect upon music. See pp. 35–36.

Esfahah was reputedly larger than seventeenth-century Paris, having "162 mosques, 48 religious colleges, 1802 *caravanserai* [caravan hotels] and 273 public baths!"[16] Diplomatic relations with European countries were established during the reign of Shah Abbas, Persia being a rather natural ally in Europe's conflict with the Ottoman Empire; and now the flora, fauna, and court life of Persia were subject to detailed reports from adventurous diplomats and travelers. Yet in spite of his capacities for ruling and building, Shah Abbas did not plan well for his succession. He had so subordinated his sons during his rule (either by blinding or by murdering them) that the Safavid line declined. One century later the strength of the country was at a minimum, and invasion of Iran by the Afghans helped to bring about the end of the Safavid rule.

During much of the eighteenth century, Persia was ruled by two army leaders, Nader Shah Afshar and Karim Khan Zand. Nader Shah's "lightning career of conquest"[17] included the taking of Afghanistan, the sacking of Delhi, and the capture of Bukhara and Samarkand—all of which were abandoned soon after they were taken. A third military leader, Aga Mohammad Qajar, gained the throne in the closing years of the century, and it was held by his family until 1925. Throughout the Qajar reign, Persian contact with Europe increased. England, as part of her India policy, became heavily involved in Persia and thereby tangled with Russia, whose desire for a warm seaport naturally focused on her southern neighbor. Hence, Persia was a "pawn in the Anglo-Russian political game"[18] during much of the nineteenth century. Even closer contact with the West was caused by the discovery and subsequent exploitation of her great deposits of oil in the first decade of the twentieth century.

Military deposition, by now almost a tradition in modern Iran, was continued by Colonel Reza Khan, who in 1925 overthrew the last Qajar monarch to establish the present Pahlavi dynasty. In fewer than twenty years he brought about a series of

16. Donald Wilber, *Iran Past and Present* (Princeton, 1958), p. 69.
17. John Marlowe, *Iran* (London, 1963), p. 25.
18. Frye, *Iran*, p. 65.

political, social, and economic reforms that laid the basis for a modern Iran. Deposed by the British and Russians during World War II, Reza Shah was succeeded by his son Mohammad Reza Shah, the present king of Persia.

Invasions of Persia have not yet ceased. The nineteenth and twentieth centuries have seen a more peaceful but equally effective cultural penetration by the West, accelerated in recent years by Iran's involvement in World War II and by the growth of her oil industry.[19] The large numbers of foreigners residing in the country—diplomats, military advisors, businessmen, scholars, and educators—exert significant cultural influence on Iran. Furthermore, there are now more than twenty-five thousand young Iranians studying in foreign countries, who, on their return to Iran, vigorously advocate the adoption of Western technology and Western culture.

This brief summary of Persian history has emphasized lengthy periods of foreign domination alternating with periods of native Persian rule. According to the Persians, their national character has been shaped by many centuries of war and instability, making them pessimistic and mystical. And so is their music.

In connection with the study of Persian history a further observation can be made that is equally relevant to a study of music: the remarkable continuity of Persian culture. Historians stress that, even when thoroughly dominated by the Arabs or later the Turks, Persia was, in fact, the *cultural* conqueror, repeatedly imposing her more advanced civilization on that of her invaders. Side by side with this cultural strength, however, is a trend in the opposite direction—a predilection for adopting certain foreign customs and styles. This trend is not new to the last two centuries, when Iran has emulated the West, but was noted by an earlier observer. As far back as the fifth century B.C., Herodotus remarked that "no race is so ready to adopt foreign ways as the Persian."[20]

Today, predilection for foreign ways seems to be the dominant

19. The term *peaceful* must be qualified. Although Iran never lost its sovereignty to become a colony of another country during this period, it was occupied by British, Russians, and Americans during World War II.

20. Herodotus, *The Histories*, trans. Aubrey de Sélincourt (Baltimore, Md., 1954), p. 70.

trend, causing many observers to fear a complete disappearance of traditional Persian culture in this century. Yet because these opposing tendencies—the preserving of traditional culture and the adopting of aspects of a foreign one—have offset each other in Persia for at least two thousand years, one might expect a reaction in favor of traditional Persian ways. In the areas of art and literature, this is indeed the case.[21]

A HISTORY OF PERSIAN MUSIC

Tracing Persian music history through so many centuries is a highly problematical task. For unlike the visual and literary arts, which can be studied from surviving works and fragments, there are virtually no examples of the art of music until the modern period. That the music was almost never written down is understandable, however. Since traditional Persian music is improvised, exact transmission of the repertory was far less important than in Western music. And because most teaching was done by rote, no one needed a score. Hence, although alphabetic systems for the notation of music existed in Islamic countries at least as early as the ninth century, they were seldom used. In Persia notation did not become common until the second quarter of the twentieth century, and many Persian musicians still cannot read music.

Because the actual music is lacking, secondary sources must be consulted concerning older Persian art music. For the ancient period these are largely inadequate, because narrations of historians give only brief descriptions of the instruments used in battles, and the chronicles of the royal courts are equally unenlightening. In the medieval period, particularly from the tenth to the thirteenth centuries, records and treatises are more abundant. But the textual problems here are formidable, making this period no less difficult. Some of these have been exposed by the work of the Scottish orientalist Henry Farmer (1882–1964), whose prodigious writings discuss nearly every known manuscript

21. Ehsan Yar-Shater, "The Modern Literary Idiom," Karim Amami, "Modern Persian Painting," and Ella Zonis, "Classical Persian Music in the 1960's," in *Iran Faces the Seventies*, ed. Ehsan Yar-Shater (New York, 1971), pp. 284–320, 341–348, and 365–380 respectively.

relating to Near Eastern music.[22] Farmer notes that in translating medieval Arabic, one is constantly confronted "by vague definitions which make precise interpretation difficult."[23] Thus, despite Farmer's work and the translations of the major treatises into French by Baron Rudolph d'Erlanger,[24] large portions of the treatises remain incomprehensible.

Between the early Islamic period and the modern period exists another hiatus in the sources, perhaps due to the Mongol invasions of Persia, which could have destroyed some musical treatises written in the late medieval period. And for the Safavid era writings about music, if there were any, have not yet been made available.[25] Only for the late nineteenth and early twentieth centuries are sources plentiful and problems of interpretation relatively minor. The primary and secondary sources for this period, however, exist only in the Persian language; until now they have not been interpreted by non-Iranian musicologists.

But even where records and treatises are available, it is difficult to ascertain exactly how the music of the past relates to the music performed today. Comparisons can be made with a fairly high degree of certainty concerning the intensity of musical activity in certain periods, the prevalent attitudes toward music, and the contents of musical treatises; but the music itself cannot be compared without either notated examples or performances. And despite the likelihood that Persian music was much more stable over long historical periods than was Western music, exact comparisons remain conjectural.[26]

Ancient Period: Achaemenid, Greek, and Sassanian empires
(6th century B.C. *to 7th century* A.D.*)*

Because descriptions of Achaemenid music have not yet been found in native Persian sources, they must be obtained from

22. Sixty-one of Farmer's publications are listed in the bibliography.

23. Henry G. Farmer, *Saᶜadyah Gaon on the Influence of Music* (London, 1943), p. 70.

24. *La musique arabe*, 6 vols. (Paris, 1930–1959).

25. The Iranian music student M. Bostani, presently searching Tehran libraries and private collections for manuscripts on music, has found several works from the Safavid and early Qajar periods.

26. It is likely that Iranian culture possessed that degree of inherent conservatism that produces a condition of artistic stasis. See Leonard B. Meyer, *Music, the Arts, and Ideas* (Chicago, 1967), p. 98.

the writings of the ancient Greek historians. Herodotus, an observer of the Graeco–Persian wars, mentions the chanting of the Magi priests during a sacrifice.[27] Xenophon, Athenaeus, and Strabo also offer descriptions of Persian military music.[28] Both Greek and Roman historians chronicle the musical activities of the long period between the fall of the Achaemenid empire (330 B.C.) and the rise of the Sassanians (A.D. 226). The military nature of the contact of these great empires has limited the accounts of music to that of the armies and the singing girls who accompanied the Persian troops. From the Parthian period, hymns and epic poetry have survived, but there is as yet no information on the music accompanying either literary form.[29]

These sources do little more than indicate the existence of Persian music during this early period, offering no information on either music theory or practice. This is unfortunate, for the ancient period is particularly intriguing in view of the possible connections between Greek and Persian music. During the Achaemenid period, the Persians occupied sections of Greek Asia Minor and made several forays into mainland Greece. In return, the Greeks invaded Persia, and the first great Persian empire was conquered by Alexander. During the Seleucid period (fourth to third century B.C.), the Greeks founded cities in Persia, colonized them, and intermarried with Persian women. Moreover, the Hellenization of Persian culture did not end at the close of this era but continued during the Parthian period (third century B.C. to third century A.D.).[30]

Significant musical interchange likely occurred during this extensive period of contact between Greece and Persia. Although no fragments of music exist to document the interchange, it is strongly suggested by the many similarities between contemporary Persian music and what is known of ancient Greek music.

27. Herodotus, *Histories*, p. 69.

28. Henry G. Farmer, "An Outline History of Music and Music Theory," in *A Survey of Persian Art*, ed. Arthur U. Pope and Phyllis Ackerman, 6 vols. (Oxford, 1939), III, 2785.

29. See Mary Boyce, *The Manichean Hymn Cycles in Parthian* (Oxford, 1954), and George Rawlinson, *Parthia* (London, 1893), p. 178. Iconographic sources for the history of Persian music—in this case, rock carvings, miniature paintings, and representations of musicians on pottery and metal work—will be discussed in the section of musical instruments in chapter 5.

30. Romain Ghirshman, *Iran* (Baltimore, Md., 1954), pp. 229–230.

Both musics are monophonic with some use of heterophony; both are improvised using melody types (nomoi and dastgah); and both are built on tetrachordal systems. If the connection between ancient Greek and Persian music could be substantiated, the study of contemporary Persian music with its readily available examples might be invaluable to an understanding of ancient Greek music, for which evidence is so sparse. That is, the anthropological technique of studying a tradition lost to one society but preserved in another more isolated or more conservative society, could be applied to the study of Greek music.[31]

From the Sassanian period (third to seventh century A.D.) survive the earliest native Persian sources relating to music. These give names of musicians, their activities, and descriptions of the instruments they played.[32] The most famous Sassanian musician was Barbad, court musician to King Khosros II (r. 590–628), who became legendary for his virtuosity, for the richness of his interpretations, and for some significant numbers of musical compositions and systems. Barbad is said to have written 360 banquet melodies for the king, a new one for virtually every day. He also composed thirty *lahn* and seven *Khusrovania*. What these were is unknown, but it is thought that the Khusrovania were modes, and thus Barbad is credited with inventing the Persian musical system of seven dastgah.[33] These historical data also suggest that the technique of composition by melody types can be traced as far back as the seventh century.

Medieval Period: Islamic conquest (7th to 13th centuries)
and Turko-Mongol conquest (13th to 15th centuries)

With the coming of Islam to Iran there occurred a most important confluence of two musics, Arabian and Persian. A closeness between them persisted for at least two centuries,

31. Farmer believes that during the long period of interaction between Persians and Greeks "the Greeks took more from the Orient than they gave." "Outline," p. 2785. In fact, through the early Farmer literature there runs the thread of a duel between the author and a writer on Greek music, Kathleen Schlesinger, who holds the opposite opinion. Until this area has been investigated by a dispassionate scholar familiar with both musics, one cannot tell whether this apparent similarity between the two musical cultures is the result of political and cultural interchange or stems from a common source, probably in Assyrian or Babylonian music.

32. Arthur Christensen, "La vie musicale dans la civilisation des Sassanides," *Bulletin de l'Association Française des Amis de l'Orient* 20/21 (1936).

33. A. Christensen, *L'Iran sous les Sassanides*, p. 484.

especially during the Golden Age of the Abbasid caliphate at Baghdad. At this time there was such a blending of musical styles, instruments, and terminology that the question of which music most influenced the other is still hotly debated thirteen centuries later. Historians of Persian art are fond of the doctrine that the Arabs, coming straight from the desert to a more advanced civilization in Persia, adopted the art and music of the vanquished culture. Moreover, Persian musicians claim that Persian music must have strongly influenced Arabian music because Persian musicians were favored in the Arab royal courts, Persian instruments were introduced, and a great deal of Persian musical terminology came into Arabic music. Arab musicians, on the other hand, feel that their music was the basis for Persian music because there are equally as many Arabic words used in Persian music terminology.[34]

The Islamic period produced more writings on music than any other. As a sampling, Farmer lists twenty-eight music theorists from the eighth to the twelfth centuries, claiming that these are only the "most important" and that the list excludes littérateurs and biographers.[35] But there are also numerous writings in the latter category. The monumental *Kitab al Aghani* by Abul Faraj al-Isfahani (897–967), now in a twenty-one volume edition, lists the virtuosi of the period and the music they played—a sort of Grove's dictionary of the day![36] Finally, apart from theoretical and historical writings, there are many vehement religious discussions concerning the illegality of music in Islam and equally many tracts written in defense of music.[37]

34. This emphasis on national claims in Islamic music has been carried to extremes. For example, of the four most renowned music theorists of this period, three—al-Farabi, Ibn Sina, and Safi al-Din—are simultaneously claimed by Persians, Arabs, Turks, and even Russians on the basis of their birthplace, lineage, place of residence, or the language of their works.

35. Henry G. Farmer, *Historical Facts for the Arabian Musical Influence* (London, 1930), pp. 27–28.

36. Leiden, 1868–1888. Al-Isfahani's name suggests that either he or his family was Persian. His work is also important for its listing of the names of modes beside the verses of song. For extensive quotations from the *Kitab al Aghani*, see Julian Ribera, *Music in Ancient Arabia and Spain*, trans. and abr. Eleanor Hague and Marion Leffingwell (London, 1929).

37. See M. L. Roychoudhury, "Music in Islam," *Journal of the Royal Asiatic Society* 23 (1957), 47–102.

From records of musical activity in the royal courts, it appears that some caliphs, while awaiting the outcome of the theological disputes, actively championed music.[38] A few of these rulers were musicians themselves, and during their reigns, royal patronage of music was considerable. Among the musicians in the court of the Abbasid caliphs, two of the most celebrated were of Persian descent: Ibrahim al-Mausili (d. 804), who was patronized by Harun al-Rashid, and his son Ishaq al-Mausili (767–850).

The imposing body of theoretical writings on music is by far the most significant achievement in this period of Islamic music. These treatises appeared as part of the extensive scientific writings produced in Baghdad; and since music was then considered a science, part of the quadrivium to be studied along with arithmetic, astronomy, and geometry, it was included in these works. In fact the four principal Islamic music theorists—al-Kindi, al-Farabi, Ibn Sina, and Safi al-Din—were philosophers whose writings cover vast areas of thought, political and metaphysical as well as scientific.[39] Characteristic of these works is the strong influence of ancient Greek music theory. The Islamic treatises appear to be modeled on the works of Euclid, Aristoxenus, and other Greek treatises that were translated into Arabic during the ninth century. This association with the Greek theorists is acknowledged by Safi al-Din in the introduction to his *Sharaffiya* treatise: "Ceci est une épître qui comprend la science des rapports harmoniques exposée selon une méthode établie par les anciens sages de la Grèce."[40]

The first of the leading Islamic music theorists, founder of the school of "philosopher scientists,"[41] is the Arab al-Kindi (ca. 801–866). Only four of his seven reported treatises have survived, and one of these contains the first musical notation found in Arab sources.[42]

Al-Farabi, known in Europe as Alpharabius, was born at Wasij, Farab, in the province of Transoxiana (now the area east of the

38. Henry G. Farmer, *A History of Arabian Music* (London, 1929), p. 104.
39. Their music treatises in French translation are in *MA*.
40. D'Erlanger, *MA*, III, 3.
41. Hossein Nasr, *Three Muslim Sages* (Cambridge, Mass. 1964), p. 9.
42. Farmer, *Historical Facts*, pp. 312–314.

Caspian Sea in the Soviet Union). He completed his studies in Baghdad and resided in Aleppo from 941 until his death in 950. Like many philosophers of the time, al-Farabi lived the life of a Sufi.[43] His writings cover many fields of thought, including politics; and for his work in defining and systematizing the science of his day, he is called the "second master," Aristotle being considered the "first master." During the twelfth century, many works of al-Farabi, translated into Latin, were used in European universities.[44] Among his several works on music, the greatest is the *Kitab al musiqi al Kabir* (Grand Book on Music) in which he discusses every known aspect of music.

Unlike most philosophers of the period, who spent a good portion of their lives in the Abbasid capital, the greatest of them did not work at Baghdad but spent most of his life in Persia. Ibn Sina (Avicenna, 980–1037) was born in Central Asia, traveled across Khorassan in eastern Iran, and lived in Ray, which is near Tehran, and then in Esfahan. He died in the city of Hamadan in western Iran, where his tomb may be visited today. During his lifetime he was most famous as a doctor, but also spent time in political life. A recent study of Ibn Sina reports that his extant writings, which number close to two hundred fifty, deal with every subject known to the medieval world—logic, psychology, cosmology, metaphysics, meteorology, zoology, geology, and medicine.[45] Comprising a very small part of this corpus, his writings on music are found in the *al Shifa* (Book of the Remedy) and the *Najat* (Book of Deliverance).[46] Unlike al-Farabi, Ibn Sina was not a practical musician, and more information on the practice of eleventh-century music is contained in the writings of his contemporary Ibn Zaila (d. 1048).[47]

The last theorist of the magnitude of al-Farabi and Ibn Sina—

---

43. Nasr, *Three Muslim Sages*, p. 16.

44. According to Farmer, eight of the works of al-Farabi were translated into Latin. Farmer has edited two of them in *Al Farabi's Arabic–Latin Writings on Music* (Glasgow, 1934). See also E. A. Beichert, "Die Wissenschaft der Musik bei al-Farabi," *Kirchenmusikalisches Jahrbuch* 27 (1932).

45. Nasr, *Three Muslim Sages*, pp. 23–24.

46. These two works of Ibn Sina on music were translated into Latin at Toledo during the twelfth century. Farmer, *Historical Facts*, p. 37.

47. Farmer, "Outline," p. 2793.

in fact, for Persian music as distinct from Arabian, the most significant of the four—is the thirteenth-century writer Safi al-Din al-Mumin (d. 1294).[48] Born at Urmiya, in the Persian province of Azerbaijan, Safi al-Din lived during a critical historical period: he was in the service of the last Abbasid caliph as well as the first Mongol ruler. The story is told that when Hulagu, grandson of Genghis Khan, was sacking Baghdad and slaughtering its inhabitants, he heard of this famous musician. Commanded to play before the Mongol conqueror, Safi al-Din so impressed Hulagu that his life was spared. From 1258 Safi al-Din was in the service of the Mongol court, and one of his great works on music, the *Sharaffiya* treatise, is dedicated to Sharaf al-Din Harun, son of Hulagu's vazir. Persian theorists throughout the late medieval period and even in the modern period have relied on the works of Safi al-Din, the *Risalat ash Sharaffiya* and the *Kitab ad Advar*.[49]

The Persians continued to produce treatises on music during the Turko-Mongol period, but after Safi al-Din, the language was mainly Persian, rather than Arabic. In the fourteenth century, Qutb [sic] al-Din al-Shirazi (d. 1310), a pupil of Safi Al-Din, wrote what is perhaps the most abstruse mathematical treatise on music, the *Durat ol Taj*.[50] Ali al-Jurgani (d. 1413), is the author of a well-known commentary on the works of Safi al-Din.[51] The end of the line of illustrious theorists is reached with Abd Qadir Ghaibi al Maraghi (d. 1435), whose works were

---

48. Among the numerous treatises written between the works of Ibn Sina and Safi al-Din are the *Encyclopedia of the Brothers of the Purity* (Ilkwan al-Safa), the works of Fakhr al-Din al-Razi, 1149–1209, written in Persian, not Arabic, and those of Nasir al-Din al-Tusi, 1201–1274. See Farmer, *Sources*, pp. 34–50.

49. An important but problematic treatise on music which is signed with the name of Safi al-Din and written in Persian is the *Bahjat al Ruh*^c (Gladness of the Soul). In 1937, Henry Farmer asked the Persian specialist Rabino de Borgomale to edit and to translate the two manuscripts of this work that are in the British Museum and Bodleian libraries. In the process of this work, Borgomale came to the opinion that the author was not the famed Safi al-Din, but a lesser writer masking his own work under the name of the celebrated theorist. Borgomale and other Persian advisers, on the basis of internal evidence, have assigned this work to the opening of the seventeenth century. This, in fact, makes it a more interesting document, as we have very few Persian sources from this later period. The completed edition in manuscript and the translation, both done by Borgomale, now in the Senate Library in Tehran, were put at my disposal through the kindness of Jahan Dori, senate librarian. See Appendix 2 for excerpts from this treatise. The manuscript has been published by the Cultural Foundation of Iran (Tehran, 1346 [1965]).

50. Farmer, *Sources*, p. 51. He does not mention that the *Durat ol Taj* is available in modern edition (Tehran, 1324 [1945]).

51. D'Erlanger, *MA*, III.

circulated widely throughout the Middle East.[52] His *Jami al Alhan* contains the first extensive examples of notated Persian music. Maraghi provides a connection between Persian and Turkish music, for he served the Ottoman ruler Bayazid I, and his son and grandson produced treatises in the service of later Turkish sultans.

Two features of the Mongol period that are important to music history should be carefully differentiated. One was the practice of the court at Samarkand to encourage artists and men of letters, thus producing a brilliant period in Persian art. The other was the inordinate amount of destruction caused by these same Mongul rulers. To conquer and hold their empires, they sacked cities, destroyed valuable libraries, ruined agricultural systems, and slaughtered populations. This second aspect of Mongul history left an undocumented, but nonetheless real legacy to Persian music. Not only did it provide the stimulus for the great mystic poetry written at this time, it also helped to mold the serious character and emotional outlook of the Persians.

Renaissance Period: Safavid dynasty (16th to early 18th centuries)

After many centuries of foreign domination, the Safavid dynasty produced a renaissance of Persian culture that lasted from the sixteenth to the eighteenth centuries. But whereas examples of Safavid architecture and fine arts are well known, it appears that this period did not encourage a flourishing of music. Strangely enough, the Safavid period is one of the low points in the history of Persian music. This artistic hiatus, quite unexpected and at first inexplicable, might well be due to the religious climate of the period.[53] In their attempts to solidify the country and to create an independent political unit, the Safavid rulers reemphasized religion, which had been relatively absent from politics since before the tenth century. The Safavids made the Shiʿa branch of Islam the official religion of Persia, and, in fact, recreated the independent nation on its basis. The religious emphasis in the Safavid period served to bring to the fore that disapprobation

---

52. Farmer, *Sources*, p. 59.
53. For this hypothesis, I am grateful to Ruhollah Khaleqi.

of music always latent in Islam. Moreover, it is not unlikely that at this time religion had a more profound influence on the whole society than it did during the height of the great Islamic period of the eighth, ninth, and tenth centuries, when music often flourished side by side with the religious debates against it. The difference might be explained by the differing attitudes of the royal court. Whereas the Abbassids ruled an empire already firmly established on a religious basis, the Safavids felt an urgent need to wield religion as an instrument of national policy. To this end, they encouraged religious writings as well as the creation of religious legalities and dogma (*Khorofat*) and opposed the deviancy of the Sufis, the main supporters of music.[54]

In such a religious country as Persia, and especially at this intensely religious time, what the clergy ordained and the royal court sanctioned was closely followed. Music lost its social approval, a condition that lasted well into the twentieth century. But even more damaging than the accompanying loss of patronage was its loss of respectability as a profession. In Safavid Persia, music became the province of illiterate entertainers, who were accorded the rank of laborer and in contemporary accounts are even called "laborers of pleasure."[55] Among the upper classes, those with musical talent who might otherwise have become professionals remained amateurs, practicing their art in private. Indeed, the Safavid rulers so thoroughly suppressed the musical profession that even after the dynasty was firmly established and religious control relaxed, social disapproval of music remained,

---

54. Edward G. Browne, examining the reason for the corresponding dearth of great literature at this time in Persia, received the following suggestion from a Persian friend: "Now although these divines strove greatly to effect the religious unification of Persia (which resulted in its political unification), and laid the foundations of this present-day Persia . . . from the point of view of literature, Poetry, Sufiism, and mysticism . . . they not merely fell short in the promotion thereof, but sought by every means to injure and annoy the representatives of these 'accomplishments,' who were generally not too firmly established in the Religious Law and its derivatives. In regard to the Sufiis particularly they employed every kind of severity and vexation, whether by exile, expulsion, slaughter or reprimand, slaying or burning many of them with their own hands or by their sentence. Now the close connection between poetry and Belles Lettres on the one hand, and Sufiism and Mysticism on the other, at any rate in Persia, is obvious, so that the extinction of one necessarily involves the extinction and destruction of the other. Hence it was that under this dynasty learning, culture, poetry and mysticism completely deserted Persia." *A Literary History of Persia*, 6 vols. (Cambridge, 1928), IV, 26–27.

55. Khaleqi, "*Amaleh tarab*," *SMI*, p. 23.

in marked contrast to the honoring of musicians in Sassanian times and to the great respect the musical profession held during the early Islamic period.[56] Today, a legacy of the Safavid attitude can be discerned in the lesser respect accorded to music practice as compared with theory—in the prevalent attitude that "music is good when it is scientific, but playing is not good."[57] This theme is also found in many present-day writings that mourn the loss of science in music with the passing of Safi al-Din in the thirteenth century, or Maraghi in the fifteenth, and declare the following centuries to be a dark age in Persian music until Vaziri reestablished Persian music on a scientific basis in 1923.[58]

The sources for accounts of music during the Safavid and early Qajar periods are remarkably sparse. Henry Farmer, in his detailed history of Persian music, mentions these source peculiarities—the lack of native histories and treatises—but he seems to gloss over this apparent decline in music. For example, he quotes three treatises "probably" from the sixteenth century, but does not explain their sudden anonymity. Another trend that he recounts but does not rationalize is the sudden reappearance of "defenses" of music during the seventeenth century.[59]

But despite Safavid politics, Persian music was still brilliant during this period—not in Persia but in India. The Mogul emperors, descendants of Tamerlane who ruled North India until they

56. In an eleventh-century handbook that a Persian prince wrote for his son, the profession of musician is treated in equal detail and with the same respect as that of statesman or scientist. Kai Ka'us Ibn Iskandar, *Qabus Nama: A Mirror for Princes*, trans. Reuben Levy (London, 1951), pp. 186–190. Contemporary attitudes toward music and musicians are a contrast. "If a musician's life has never been a glamorous one in Iran it has had the added disadvantage of being victimized by social prejudice ("*motreb*" still carries a perjorative connotation) and a general sense of self-pity." Parry Ebrahimzadeh. *Kayhan International* (7 November 1967), p. 4. "Another influence of religion is seen in the neglect of music. Not that the Persians are not sensitive to music—far from that. In fact, all Persian poetry may be sung, and all the poets speak of their love for music. But the Islamic tradition repudiates music, and the clergy have always discouraged singing and playing on musical instruments. Out of that tradition has grown a contempt, not for music itself, but for those who perform it. It seemed unworthy and degrading to take part in any musical entertainment." Issa Khan Sadiq, *Modern Persia and Her Educational System* (New York, 1931).

57. Ruhollah Khaleqi, in conversation.

58. For example, the publication *Iran Almanac 1962* (Tehran, 1962), p. 863.

59. Farmer, "Outline," p. 2801. It is quite likely that more writings exist than have presently been mentioned in the literature. Neither Henry Farmer nor other scholars of Persian music seem to have investigated the numerous Persian manuscripts that Richard Frye informed me are catalogued in Russian libraries.

were supplanted by the British, brought their culture with them from Central Asia. Although the Moguls themselves were Turks, their courtly culture was Persian, and Persian was the language of diplomacy and literature.[60] The best-known examples of this cultural transplantation are the many Persian-style buildings in India, among them the Taj Mahal, and the numerous miniature paintings in a Persian style produced in India.[61] Accounts of music from this period show that as in the other arts, Persian influence was considerable. Abu Fazl, court chronicler to the important Mogul monarch Akbar (r. 1556–1605), mentions several Persians in his list of court musicians. He also gives an extensive account of the nagareh khaneh at Delhi.[62]

Traces of Persian influence are evident in present-day Indian music. There is a vast correspondence in terminology; for example, some Indian names of instruments—tambura, sitar, dohol, nuy, surnai, nafari, naqara, and tabla—and names of forms and styles—gazal, tarana, durbari—appear to have a Persian origin. Indian writers themselves feel that the Persian influence, which was also considerable in earlier centuries than the Mogul period, especially the thirteenth and fourteenth, was responsible for the bifurcation of Indian music into Hindustani and Carnatic styles.[63] Some of the technical features that differentiate North Indian music from South Indian music are familiar style characteristics of Persian music: the greater use of decoration, the lesser reliance on fixed compositions, and the less mathematical rhythm.[64] That the theories of both Indian and Persian music overlap at many points—the use of melody types, the division of

60. Edward G. Browne mentions the movement of Persian poets to Delhi at this time owing to the more liberal policies of the Moguls toward literature. *Literary History*, IV, 28.

61. Examples of these paintings may be seen in J. Marek and H. Knizkova, *The Jenghiz Khan Miniatures from the Court of Akbar the Great* (London, 1963).

62. Abul Fazl, *Ain i Akbari*, trans. H. Blochman. This selection is found in S. M. Tagore, ed., *Hindu Music from Various Authors* (Calcutta, 1875), pp. 211–216.

63. An important article on the Islamic influence in music during these centuries is Dharma Bhanu, "The Promotion of Music by the Turko-Afghan Rulers of India," *Islamic Culture* 29 (January 1955), 9–31.

64. The Indian writer O. Gosvami states that "Hindu art in general impresses us in mass, with its sublimity, strength and poise, while Mohammedan art specialized in grace and decorative details ... With the cultural impact of the Muslims, Hindu music acquired a decorative element." *The Story of Indian Music* (Bombay, 1957), p. 275.

the octave into twenty-two microtones—suggests an even earlier musical relationship, perhaps originating during the period when Greece governed parts of both Iran and northwest India.

Modern Period (late 18th to 20th centuries)

During the late eighteenth and early nineteenth centuries, music slowly began to regain its social respectability. In contrast to the Safavid period, there are now accounts of music from Persian writers, among them Ahmad Mirza Azadih Dowleh, one of the many sons (fifty-seven!) of the second Qajar ruler, Fath Ali Shah (r. 1797–1834). In his history, *Tarikh-e Azudi*, he lists the names of musicians and also reports on their activities in the royal court.[65] In the second half of the nineteenth century, Western music was formally introduced into Persia. Nasir ed Din Shah (r. 1848–1896), most impressive of the Qajar monarchs, imported a French musicmaster in 1858 to train his *corps de musique*. The third Frenchman to hold this position, Alfred J. B. Lemaire, founded a school of music that became important for the training of military band players and music administrators. This music school, still in existence, is now the chief conservatory in Tehran.

The most recent period in Persian music history, the so-called Constitutional period, includes the last three Qajar rulers and the two members of the present Pahlavi dynasty. This period is well documented and reported by Ruhollah Khaleqi in his three-volume study *Sargozasht-e Musiqi-ye Iran*.[66] Dominating the musical scene during the Constitutional period are two Persian musicians, Mirza Abdullah (d. 1917) and Ali Naqi Vaziri (b. 1886). Abdullah is the most significant figure in the area of dastgah music, for he collected and classified all the melodies that formed the basis of classical Persian music from at least the middle of the nineteenth century. The radif of Mirza Abdullah, passed down from his father, Ali Akbar Farhani, is considered

---

65. Khaleqi, *SMI*, p. 18. See also chapter 7.
66. Volumes I and II were published at Tehran in 1954 and 1955. Volume III exists in serial form in the magazine *Musik-e Iran* nos. 89–97 (October 1959–June 1960).

to be the basis of the mainstream tradition of classical Persian music.[67] The musical contribution of Ali Naqi Vaziri is quite different from that of Abdullah, which may be considered one of conservation. Vaziri set out to modernize Persian music. For this purpose he adapted Western staff notation to Persian music, established a conservatory to train musicians in Persian music as well as Western music (the other conservatory in Tehran taught only Western music), and wrote countless compositions using Iranian melodies harmonized in a Western style.

Since the beginning of the twentieth century, the quiescence of Persian music has ended, and a new period of growth has begun, encouraged by a gradual relaxation of religious restrictions and the commencement of extensive government patronage. A further stimulus to music in Persia is the widespread popularity of Western music and musical instruments. Although the social and religious disapprobation of music still exists to a certain degree, it is no longer a serious hindrance to the development of Persian music. The future of Persian music now depends upon using these extremely powerful stimuli—state patronage and the techniques of Western music—to re-create rather than to destroy a fragile musical culture.

67. The work of Mirza Abdullah is discussed by Khatchi Khatchi in *Der Dastgah* (Regensburg, 1963).

2   The Theory of Persian Art Music

Having examined the setting of Persian music—its place in history and in contemporary times—we turn now to the music itself, proceeding, as it were, from the ecology of Persian music to its morphology. Since art is an ordering of nature, and music is an ordering of sound, a study of a music aims first to discover that order and then to explain it. One asks what system is organizing the sound that he experiences as music, or, more technically, what is the form of the music? To answer these questions, analysis is used, a process that requires us to examine the music closely and search for its order, a process that, if successful, will reward the analyst with a greater understanding and appreciation of the musical system.

When approaching a new music, especially an Oriental music so vastly different in style and structure from Western music, a Western musicologist soon finds his customary methods of analysis insufficient. This music cannot be profitably analyzed in terms of eighteenth-century tonal harmony; likewise, searching for forms common to recent Western music, for example, sonata and rondo or even simple binary and ternary forms, would be relatively futile. Certainly harmonic and formal analogies do exist, but they are clearly of minor importance. Therefore, the Western musicologist must work out a new methodology for analysis that considers the music's own particular logic and organization. He is fortunate if a music has been studied by theorists native to its country of origin and if a utilizable framework and a terminology already exist.

For the past thousand years, Persian music has rarely been at a loss for theoretical explanation. Indeed, this music has been analyzed in inordinate detail by some of the greatest thinkers of the Middle Ages. Moreover, in contemporary Persia, theoretical speculation continues. Yet, from the viewpoint of a non-Persian musicologist, the work of Persian theorists is too greatly isolated from practice. Native systems have not come to grips with the music's primary methodological problem, which is this: how can one analyze a music that changes with each performer and even with the same performer on different occasions? Because Persian music is improvised, the form of any given performance, that is, that order or organization of sound, is far less certain than the order of a given piece of Western music, which, with certain reservations stemming from interpretation and slight differences in the sources, is the same each time it is played. But whereas improvisation is such a natural and almost intuitive procedure for the Persian theorist that he does not feel the need to explain it, for the foreign musicologist, an analysis that omits the subject of improvisation is quite an incomplete one.

One solution to the problem of analyzing an improvised music is to set aside the complete performance and study the material used as a basis for improvisation. By isolating the relatively stable and unchangeable part of the performance, that is, the dastgah, or melody type, one can deal with a body of music stable enough to analyze. Then, after the investigator becomes familiar with this basic material, it can be studied within the context of the total performance. In other words, once the model for improvisation has been clarified, the way the model is used in performance can be investigated.

The first part of this methodological scheme, the setting aside of the improvised performance to study the structural framework on which it is based, has already been done. A quite formidable literature exists concerned solely with the theory of Persian music. Unfortunately, though, once Persian theorists have set aside the performance, they seldom return to it. The actual performance remains unexamined and often incomprehensible.

One may, with patience, read all of the medieval theoretical treatises written on Islamic music and also many of the modern ones and finish knowing little about performed music.[1] The illustrious works of al-Farabi, Ibn Sina, and Safi al-Din do not elucidate a performance of the music; they describe the physical and mathematical aspects of tone production, the intervals played, and, less often, the modes and the instruments.

But whereas medieval Islamic writers would seldom include an investigation of musical· practice in their scientific treatises, the present-day study of music has expanded its interest. Even though music is once again studied as a science—an "ology" taught in the university—its realms are not so narrowly defined. Under the influence of the physical sciences, musicology has discovered its own laboratory, which it has had all along but has been slow to recognize: the concert hall. In contrast to the study of music in the Middle Ages, contemporary musicology finds the study of performance practice an acceptable scholarly pursuit, thereby at long last bringing closer the art and the science of music, the practice and the theory.

To study Persian music according to modern rather than medieval science, the theory must be related to the practice. Therefore, after discussing the tonal materials and structure of Persian music using the customary methodology of Persian theorists, that is, the system of compound melody types or dastgah-ha, we shall return to the practice and discover how these dastgah-ha are used for improvisation. Three parts are involved in this investigation. First is theory, which as a discipline is similar to that of Western music—a consideration of systems abstracted from the music. In Persian music, however, the elements of harmony and counterpoint are much less important than those of melodic and rhythmic modes, of scales, and of intervals. The second subject, practice, involves a combination of the Western studies of composition and performance practice. A third part, which actually comes between theory and practice, does not have an exact counterpart in Western music. It is the

---

1. An exception is the recent book by Nelly Caron and Dariouche Safvate which devotes several chapters to practice. *Iran: Les traditions musicales* (Buchet/Chastel, 1966).

repertory of traditional material on which all Persian is based, the radif. The closest parallels in Western music might be the repertory of Gregorian chant used as basic melodic material for Western sacred music over many centuries, or the different stereotyped melodic and harmonic formulae used in individual style periods.

Each of the three aspects of Persian art music will be examined in a separate chapter. Chapter 2 considers the theory; chapter 3, the radif; and chapter 4, the practice of improvisation. The aspects of rhythm and form will be considered in greater detail in chapter 5.

THE DASTGAH AND ITS SUBSECTIONS, GUSHEH-HA

According to contemporary theorists, Persian art music is organized into twelve systems called *dastgah*, a frequently used Persian word meaning "apparatus," "mechanism," "scheme," or "organization."[2] Just as there is a dastgah for conducting government operations, for receiving radio programs, or for weaving rugs, there are dastgah-ha for making music.

The seven main dastgah of contemporary Persian art music are: Shur, Mahur, Homayun, Sehgah, Chahargah, Nava, and Rast Panjgah. In addition, there are five smaller systems which are considered auxiliary dastgah-ha. These satellite systems, four belonging to the dastgah of Shur and one to Homayun, are designated by the terms *avaz* (song) or *naghmeh* (melody). Their individual names are: Abu Ata, Bayat-e Tork, Afshari, and Dashti, associated with the dastgah of Shur; and Esfahan, associated with Homayun. For the present, these five smaller dastgah need not be differentiated from the seven main dastgah, as the hierarchic relations of all twelve systems, the dastgah-ha and the naghmeh-ha, will be considered in the next chapter.

Whereas a literal translation of the word *dastgah* as "apparatus" aptly describes the Persian musical system, Persian music theorists usually translate dastgah as "mode." The term *mode* does give the

---

2. The derivation of dastgah is from *dast*, meaning "hand", and *gah*, meaning "time" or "position."

foreign musicologist a reference point. At the same time, however, it is misleading, because a Persian dastgah is more than a
mode in the sense that the Western church modes are understood.
Like a mode, each dastgah has its own seven-note scale, and some
notes have special significance within that scale. But in addition,
each dastgah has its own special repertory of melodies called
gusheh-ha (singular gusheh), which embody the most characteristic aspects of the dastgah. When a performer is asked to define a
certain dastgah, he does not play its scale, but its first gusheh.

To create a composition the performer puts several gusheh-ha
together, usually following a traditional order that involves
an increasingly higher range for successive gusheh-ha: the first
few gusheh-ha fill the lower half of the octave; the next few fill
the rest of the octave; and later gusheh-ha may rise to the beginning of the second octave. The differences in range of four important gusheh in the dastgah of Shur are shown in Example 1
(the note shown as a quarter note receives the most stress in the
melody).

EXAMPLE I.

Daramad   Shahnaz   Salmak   Hosseini

The subdivision of the dastgah into gusheh-ha is also illustrated
in the following diagram. Here the bottom horizontal line
represents the lowest note of the octave and the upper line is the
note one octave higher. Each rectangular unit is a gusheh. The
dotted line that descends to the tonic to the right of the gusheh

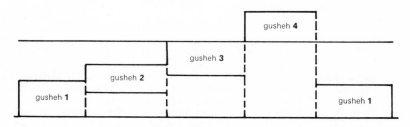

Figure 2.

represents the forud (descent), a short melody frequently played at the conclusion of a gusheh to connect it to the parent dastgah. The melody of the forud is especially characteristic of the main dastgah and always returns to main cadence note of the dastgah.

Playing the gusheh-ha of a dastgah, or "going to its corners," as the process is described in Persian, is a technique somewhat analogous to modulation. As the different gusheh-ha are played, fresh tonal areas unfold and new accidentals may be introduced. The rise in tessitura during the successive gusheh-ha helps to increase excitement, which is only momentarily released by the occasional descent to the starting point in the forud.

Because the gusheh-ha are the musical materials used as models for improvised composition, each gusheh is actually more than what a Western musician thinks of as melody. What is important is not the gusheh as a tune but, in a sense, the gusheh as genetic materials for the creation of new pieces. The genetic materials provided by the gusheh are: the modal and rhythmic features of the melody, its shape, and other features of mood and character that may be the sum of the above plus other, indefinable ingredients, such as extramusical associations. Using this material, the performer improvises a number of small pieces that, when collected, form the gusheh, one of the movements of a dastgah composition.

Thus, each gusheh is in itself a musical system, an apparatus the musician uses to create a composition. Like the Indian raga, the Arabian maqam, and the echos of Byzantine music, a gusheh is a melody type—"a traditional repertory of melodies, melodic formulae, stereotyped figures, tonal progressions, ornamentations, rhythmic patterns, etc., that serve as a model for the creation of new melodies."[3] The dastgah is a larger system, or a compound melody type.[4]

3. Willi Apel, *Harvard Dictionary of Music*, rev. ed. (Cambridge, Massachusetts, 1969), s.v. "Melody type." The concept of maqam is discussed by Ella Zonis in "Persian Music," *Improvisation in Music: East and West*, ed. Ella Zonis and Leonard B. Meyer (Chicago, forthcoming), and by Johanna Spector in "Classical ʾUd Music in Egypt with Special Reference to Maqamat," *Ethnomusicology* 14 (May 1970), 243–257.

4. The dastgah as a collection of melody types is a historically newer systematization probably dating from the eighteenth century. See the dissertation by Hormoz Farhat, "The Dastgah Concept in Persian Music" (University of California, Los Angeles, 1965; University Microfilms 66–226), pp. 37–38.

To describe the features that characterize a gusheh, let us begin with its range. Most gusheh-ha are confined to a four- or five-note compass located in a specific part of the octave. Thus, a gusheh occupying the lower tetrachord does not often use notes of the upper tetrachord.[5] Another basic feature of the gusheh is the configuration of the notes within its range. If the range is a tetrachord, which is true of a majority of gusheh-ha, the tetrachord may contain either a major, minor, or neutral second, and either a major, minor, or neutral third.[6] The hierarchy of the notes in its range is an additional distinguishing feature of the gusheh. The most important notes are the one on which the melody stops, and the one that receives special emphasis in the gusheh, or occurs most often, comparable to the finalis and reciting tone of Gregorian chant. These notes have been recognized and labeled by Persian theorists: the note of stopping is the ist (stop), and the note of stress is the shahed (witness).[7] These notes are comparable to the finalis and reciting tone of Gregorian chant. The location of these preferential tones within the range of the gusheh serves to give the gusheh its particular character. For example, if two gusheh have the same range, say C to F, and one cadences on E, stressing the note F, whereas the other both cadences and stresses the note C, the two will obviously be quite different. All these factors pertaining to the range of the gusheh— its location, configuration, and hierarchy of notes—may be considered modal features of the gusheh. These are the most important characteristics of each gusheh and are well defined in the theoretical literature.

In addition to its modal characteristics, the gusheh has other features that are not so clearly definable. One is a certain melodic shape that remains recognizable throughout the improvisation.[8]

---

5. In practice, however, this limitation is not strictly observed. Octave transposition is used as a means of variation, and coloratura passages often transcend the bounds of the traditional range.

6. These intervals would be the following using C as the starting note: the seconds, C to D, C to D-flat, and C to D-koron; the thirds, C to E, C to E-flat, and C to E-koron. The koron is a nonexact half-flat.

7. Some theorists also include the note on which the gusheh starts, aqaz (start), among the notes of importance. The dastgah itself is characterized by a shahed and an ist which are the shahed and ist of the first gusheh, the daramad. In addition, the dastgah has a third note of importance, the moteghayer.

8. See below, pp. 104–115.

Another is a set of characteristic motives and cadence formulae for each gusheh. Finally, there are the extramusical associations that combine to give each gusheh an individual character. In speaking of the opening gusheh of Shur, for example, Farhat mentions its staid character, while a later gusheh, Shahnaz, he considers emotional and exciting.[9]

The features of rhythm that contribute to the genetic material of the gusheh are far more difficult to isolate, as most gusheh-ha are non-metric and are played with a very free rhythm. For those melodies that are still associated with a particular poem, the stamp of the poetic meter is recognizable in the melody.[10] Traditional motives and ornaments used in certain gusheh-ha also bear their own rhythmic characteristics. But most of the rhythmic features of a gusheh seem specific to the performer rather than to the gusheh.[11] The tempo, on the other hand, is primarily determined by traditional usage.

A comparison of four gusheh of Shur will show how each is distinguished by those genetic features that we have discussed: the location and extent of the range of each, the configuration of the notes in its range, the notes of stress and stopping, and the melodic shape. Note that the examples indicate not what was actually played but what was abstracted by Persian theorists from improvised performances. Such condensed versions of each gusheh do not exist in practice. For the opening gusheh, the daramad (Example 2),[12] the melodic range encompasses the

EXAMPLE 2.   Ma'ruffi, *MTI*, p. 2. (g′)

tetrachord from middle C to F, with the use of the lower auxiliary, B-flat, in the final cadence. The configuration of the tetrachord

9. Farhat, "The Dastgah Concept," pp. 58–59.

10. See chapter 5.

11. This rhythmic independence may be observed in comparing the different versions of the daramad of each dastgah given in chapter 3.

12. The gusheh called daramad, the first gusheh in every dastgah, gives its name to the dastgah. Hence the daramad in this example is also called Shur. The word *daramad* is derived from *dar* (door) and *amad* (it enters).

is noteworthy as it is not comparable to any found in Western music. There are two consecutive neutral seconds: C to D-koron and D-koron to E-flat.

In the daramad, both the shahed and the ist, the notes of stress and stopping, coincide, accounting for the heavy emphasis on the note C. The melodic shape of this particular version of the daramad, which is shared by those of many other musicians, has three basic elements. The first is stressing of the tonic by repeated sounding of it and its upper auxiliary, D-koron. The second is the widening of the tonal area to three and then four notes with stress on the return to the tonic from each. The final cadence again stresses the leading-tone function of the upper auxiliary, here with the lower leading tone used for additional stress. The predominant melodic contour, especially clear in this daramad, may be described in a single word—descent.

These, then, are the basic characteristics of the daramad of Shur. When a composer employs this genetic material to create an improvised composition, these elements are used as the basis for the individual small pieces that form the sections of the gusheh. The composer whose version of the daramad was quoted, Mussa Maʿruffi, retains the modal characteristics, the basic shape of the melody, and the characteristic figures throughout the fourteen small pieces making up the gusheh.[13]

The other gusheh-ha of Shur may differ from the daramad in some or all of the essential features. The gusheh Shahnaz (Example 3), has the same modal configuration as Shur—two

EXAMPLE 3.   Khaleqi, *NM*, p. 132. (a′)

13. See chapter 4, pp. 120–125.

neutral seconds—but it is located in a higher range, the upper tetrachord, F to B-flat. We might say that it is in the same mode but a different key from the daramad. In addition, the melodic range is wider and the melodic shape more sweeping than the daramad with its constant descent to the tonic. Another gusheh, Salmak (Example 4), is located in the same tetrachord as Shahnaz,

EXAMPLE 4.   Borumand (Tsuge transcription). (g′)

yet it has not only a different melody from Shahnaz, but also a different modal structure, a major second and a minor second, and a different shahed, G instead of F. Characteristic of Salmak is the use of two forms of the note G: G-natural at the beginning and G-koron later in the gusheh. The gusheh located in the highest register of Shur is Hosseini (Example 5). Although it

EXAMPLE 5.   Farhat, p. 60. (d′)

uses the same notes as does the daramad it is sounded an octave higher. Furthermore it has a clear melodic tendency, an ascending shape, that sets its apart from the daramad and the other gusheh-ha of Shur.[14]

Thus, each of the gusheh-ha in the dastgah, distinguished by modal and melodic features, provides genetic material for the small sections of the performer's improvised composition. Returning to the schematic representation of the dastgah and its

14. Farhat, "The Dastgah Concept," p. 60.

division into gusheh-ha given above, let us further enlarge one of the rectangular units representing a gusheh. We now observe a series of small pieces that develop the melodic ideas characteristic of each gusheh.[15] The number of pieces in a particular gusheh is not fixed but varies from one to fifteen, depending upon the player and the length of the improvisation.

Figure 3.

Each gusheh in the dastgah has a descriptive title. Some names are taken from the towns, villages, or tribes from which the melodies are said to have originated. The gusheh Zabol in the dastgah Sehgah, for example, is named for a town in eastern Persia, and the gusheh Bakhtiari in Homayun is named for the large Bakhtiari tribe. Certain titles simply describe the gusheh: bozorg (big), kuchek (small); and some gusheh-ha carry the names of persons: Hosseini, Mansuri. Tracing the names of the gusheh-ha is fascinating, since some mentioned as early as the tenth century are still in use today. In addition, there are similarities in the names used in the Arabic and Turkish maqam repertories.

The total number of gusheh-ha in all twelve dastgah makes up a body of music called the radif. This is the basis of Persian art music, and Persian musicians speak of "playing the radif" rather than "playing dastgah music." Existing as a basic repertory upon which Persian art music is created, the radif may be thought of as a layer between theory and practice, for it is the radif that the performer learns as a student. Section by section he memorizes a number of gusheh-ha from each dastgah. Each section is one of the small pieces in the diagram above. In a typical lesson, the student plays one or two of the pieces he has memorized and reads through the new ones he will memorize for the next lesson. The teacher then plays the new pieces to clarify the phrase

15. The units differ slightly in height since performers frequently extend the limits of the gusheh's range with ornamental notes. How these pieces develop the melodic ideas of the gusheh will be discussed in chapter 4.

structure and the ornamentation, which are not precisely indicated in the present notation system. Today a Persian student learns
the sections of the gusheh from books, a practice dating from the
last two decades when the gusheh-ha were notated and published
by several masters; before teaching manuals became available, the
radif was learned by rote.

Because this music was unwritten for so long, the repertory of
pieces is extremely varied. The number of pieces in each gusheh
and the number of gusheh-ha within any one dastgah varies
from teacher to teacher and from publication to publication.
With each succeeding generation of performers, new gusheh-ha
enter the repertory and older ones are forgotten. Notation and
publication may tend to standardize their number and form,
however, especially the appearance of the "official radif,"
published recently by the Ministry of Art and Culture of the
Government of Iran.[16]

The form and content of any single gusheh may also differ
widely. Indeed, there is hardly a single version of any melody
accepted by all Persian musicians, for the gusheh-ha are not
finished pieces but the starting materials or the models for
improvisation.[17] Similarly, the collection of gusheh-ha, the
dastgah, is a collection of models for improvisation. As with the
dastgah-e golichi, the loom or the apparatus used for making
Persian carpets, the musical dastgah is only the apparatus the
performer uses to make music.

THE PERSIAN SCALE

A discussion of intervals and their arrangement in scale patterns
follows that of the other elements of the dastgah rather than
preceding it, as might otherwise seem logical. Unlike a Western
musician, who, when asked to describe a specific mode,
immediately thinks of its scale, a Persian musician thinks in terms
of certain melodies. These do, in fact, prescribe the succession
of tones of the dastgah, but arranging these tones into a scale is

---

16. Mehdi Barkechli and Mussa Maᶜruffi, *MTI*.

17. Variations in different versions of the radif are discussed in chapter 3, which also
illustrates variations in different versions of each gusheh.

an abstraction that the conservatory-trained musician thinks of only secondarily, and the provincial musician is usually unable to do so at all.[18] By considering the scale at this time, after the discussion of gusheh-ha, the present study of the Persian dastgah stresses the importance of the melodies (gusheh-ha) rather than the scale as the framework for composition.

Yet, although the concept of a scale is quite far removed from the thoughts of the performer, it is precisely this subject that has engrossed the theorists for centuries. The medieval treatises, especially those of Al-Farabi, Ibn Sina, and Safi al-Din, devote extensive chapters to the arrangement and sizes of the intervals in the octave. Even today, a preoccupation with intervals exists among Persian theorists.[19] It is difficult to keep a discussion of music theory to any other subject for very long before the inevitable question of intervals is hotly debated. And, following the lead of the Persians, earlier European writers have concentrated on this aspect of Persian and Arabian music, resulting in a considerable literature dealing mainly with intervals and scales in Islamic music.[20]

The scales used by Persian musicians have seven degrees, as do those used in the West. But whereas the modern Western scale is drawn from a pool of twelve notes, the scales of Persian music are extracted from a pool that contains from seventeen to twenty-four notes, depending on the theorist and his method of dividing the whole tone. The twelve notes of the Western scale result from a division of the whole tone into two parts. In the Persian music system, however, the whole tone may be divided into three or four parts rather than two. Thus, in an octave of five whole tones and two half tones (which are not further divided here), a division of the whole tones into three parts yields seventeen notes from which a scale may be drawn ($5 \times 3 + 2 = 17$). Similarly, dividing each whole tone into four units produces

---

18. Hormoz Farhat, Review of the recording *Musical Anthology of the Orient: Iran,* *Ethnomusicology* 6 (1962), 239–241.

19. One of Persia's leading musicologists is a scientist whose specialty is acoustics. Mehdi Barkechli (b. 1913) teaches both physics and musicology at the University of Tehran and has published extensively on Persian music.

20. For instance, the articles on Persian, Arabian, and Turkish music in *LavE.*

twenty-two notes, and if the two half tones are also divided into quarter tones, twenty-four notes is the result.

The method of dividing the whole tone to produce the intervals used by practicing musicians causes the chief disagreement among Persian music theorists. The following discussion, meant to contrast recent opinion rather than to raise the issue anew, will consider two methods.[21] The most direct one is to divide the whole tone into four equal parts. The intervals between C and D could then be represented as C 1/4, C 2/4, and C 3/4. Or, using the system of acoustical cents, in which a whole tone is set equal to 200 cents, a half tone to 100 cents, the intervals between C and D are 50 cents, 100 cents, and 150 cents. The dividing unit of the whole tone is, in this case, the quarter tone.

In the second system of dividing the whole tone, which is of Greek origin, the dividing units are the acoustical values of limma and comma rather than the quarter tone. The limma has a value of 90 cents; the comma, 24 cents. According to the Persian theorist Mehdi Barkechli, the whole tone C to D is divided as follows:[22]

C_1	one comma	24 cents
C_2	one limma	90 cents
C_3	one limma and one comma	114 cents
D	two limmas and one comma	204 cents

A considerable difference exists between the first intervals, C 1/4 and C_1, and the third intervals, C 3/4 and C_3, of the two systems. C 1/4 according to the quarter-tone system has a value of 50 cents; according to Barkechli, C_1 has a value of 24 cents. The interval C 3/4 in quarter tones is 150 cents; according to Barkechli, C_3 is 114 cents. This difference has occasioned a controversy of theoretical opinion among Persians and is one reason that a

---

21. See also Farhat, "The Dastgah Concept," pp. 11–29, and Caron and Safvate, *Iran*, pp. 25–37.

22. Barkechli, *MTI*, p. 22. Throughout his treatise, Barkechli uses the French system of savarts rather than cents to measure acoustical intervals. To convert the savart into an approximate value in cents, multiply by 3.9.

discussion of music theory will soon turn into a heated argument concerning intervals.[23]

For notation purposes, Ali Naqi Vaziri named and symbolized the microtones. C_1 and C 1/4 he called *sori* and designated ⯑. C_3 and C 3/4 he called *koron* and designated ⯑. In Vaziri's system, the sori is attached to the note to indicate a microtone interval above that note. Thus, C⯑ indicates one microtone above C. The koron, however, is attached to a note to indicate one microtone below that note. Thus, D⯑ indicates one microtone below D. According to the widely used Vaziri system, then, the intervals between C and D would be notated as follows:

C
C⯑   one microtone above C
C♯ or D♭   two microtones above C
D⯑   three microtones above C or one microtone below D
D

The koron appears much more frequently in today's notation of Persian music than does the sori. Without taking sides in the quarter-tone-versus-limma-comma debate, the koron may be considered a nonexact half flat or three-quarter tone in the following musical examples. D koron, for example, is located approximately half way between C-sharp/D-flat and D-natural. But, as if to confound the musicologist, this three-quarter tone is sometimes notated by using a sori. Thus, the method for indicating the three-quarter tone above C is by the symbol D⯑; the three-quarter tone above D, E⯑. But, because E to F is a half step, a three-quarter tone above E would be F⯑ or a microtone above F. Similarly, B to C is a half step so that a three-quarter tone above B would be C⯑. Given that the three-quarter tone is a major interval in Persian music, it is important to note that, depending on its position in the scale, the three-quarter tone may be indicated by a koron and by a sori.

---

23. Another difference between the two groups of theorists is that the adherents of the quarter-tone division seem to recognize that it is a rather artificial measurement and that what is played varies from player to player. Barkechli, on the other hand, believes that the intervals he has calculated are those that are actually played.

Because each whole tone can be divided into four intervals, there are five different sizes of seconds available and three sizes of thirds:

seconds		*thirds*	
minor	C to D♭	minor	C to E♭
neutral	C to Dᵖ	neutral	C to Eᵖ
major	C to D	major	C to E
neutral augmented	C to D♯		
augmented	C to D♯		

There is consequently a great number of tetrachordal species available.[24] Of course, the seven most common, transposed to start on the note C, are the following:

C	Dᵖ	E	F
C	Dᵖ	E♭	F
C	Dᵖ	Eᵖ	F
C	D♭	E	F
C	D♭	E♭	F
C	D	E♭	F
C	D	E	F

To gain a full octave, these seven types of tetrachords are combined. Again, there are many possible combinations, but a limited number is commonly used today. These are given below, again transposed to start on C, with the names of the dastgah-ha to which they belong.[25]

Mahur, Rast Panjgah	C	D	E	F	G	A	B	C
Shur, Dashti, Abu Ata	C	Dᵖ	E♭	F	G	A♭	B♭	C
Bayat-e Tork	C	D	E	F	G	A	Bᵖ	C
Afshari	C	D	Eᵖ	F	G	A⁽♭⁾	B♭	C
Homayun	C	Dᵖ	E	F	G	A♭	B♭	C

24. Cf. the Greek "shades" or *genera*.
25. The musical examples in chapter 3 use different scales for Abu Ata, Afshari, and Dashti. Reasons for the differences are given in the section preceding these examples. Differences may also be found between this version of the Persian scales and those given by other authors.

Esfahan	C	D	E♭	F	G	A^P	B$^{(P)}$	C
Sehgah	C	D^P	E^P	F	G^P	A^P	B^P	C
Chahargah	C	D^P	E	F	G	A^P	B	C
Nava	C	D	E♭	F	G	A^P	B♭	C

As was mentioned above, the basic scale used in Persian music is composed of seven notes. But just as the Western seven-note scale may be supplemented by accidentals, so too may the Persian scale. For each dastgah there is usually one note of the scale that is altered during the performance for an important gusheh or several gusheh-ha. This note is called the moteghayer (changeable).[26] In the dastgah of Shur, for example, the fifth note of the scale is G-natural for the first gusheh, the daramad. But for the gusheh of Shahnaz, the G-natural is lowered to G-koron, where it remains throughout this gusheh. The note G is the moteghayer of Shur. Normally, there is but one moteghayer for each dastgah, and thus, only one principal accidental is added during the performance. This is quite different from Western music of the last three centuries which may add many accidentals to the seven notes of the scale during a single composition. Although a Persian musician is free to alter other scale degrees during the performance for expressive purposes, these ornamental notes will not remain altered for more than a short time, and they cannot be considered to have a structural function, as does the moteghayer.

That the number of accidentals added during each performance is extremely small may be demonstrated by examining the santur, one of the most popular instruments used today in Persia and the one most limited in its tuning. This zitherlike instrument is tuned for a seven-note scale (see Figure 4). For two of the seven notes, E and F, there are two sets of strings so that two notes can be sounded in each register, for example, f, f♯; f′, f♯′; f″, f♯″. But for the other five notes, C, D, G, A, and B, there is only one set of strings. Hence, in order to add an accidental to one of these notes, one of the octaves must be tuned differently before the performance: for example, g♯, g′, g″; or g, g♯′, g″; or g, g′, g♯″. This tuning results in a sudden shift of register when the player

26. The moteghayer is, like the shahed and ist, one of the notes that defines the dastgah.

sounds the altered note (see Example 6). (It is possible to move the bridges supporting the strings, but this is almost never done.)

EXAMPLE 6.   Saba, *DDS*, p. 23. (e′)

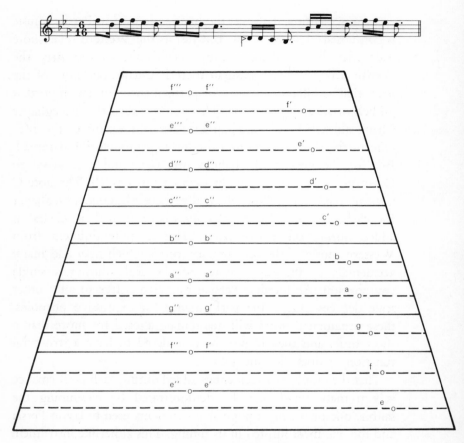

Figure 4. The Tuning of the Santur

In this schematic representation, the solid lines are the steel rings, and the broken lines, the brass. The open circles represent the bridges supporting the strings.

RHYTHM

For medieval Islamic writers, a principal branch of music theory was rhythm. Corresponding to the melodic modes or maqamat were rhythmic modes called iqaʿat. These modes and the complex notation systems used to discuss them are found in Appendix A.

Although modes similar to the medieval rhythmic modes exist today in Arabian music, they seem to have disappeared from contemporary practice in Persia. No longer formally taught, the iqaʿat are not only unknown to most Persian musicians, but they are not mentioned in recent theoretical works.[27] The rhythmic modes that do exist in Persia today concern the realm of poetry, rather than that of music, strictly speaking. But since most traditional music is vocal and uses classical poetry, the poetic modes have a direct relation to the articulation of rhythm in music and will be set forth briefly here.[28]

The study that deals with metrics is called the science of ʿaruz (prosody or meter). In the rather complicated scansion systems of Arabic and Persian poetry, the poetic feet are called avazn (weights). Those most commonly found in classical and modern Persian poetry are listed below, using two onomatopoeic systems: the first employs radicals of the Arabic verb faʿayl (to do); the second uses syllables based on "tan."

The Poetic Feet

1.	faʿūlun	فعولن	ta tan tan	∪ — —
2.	fāʿilun	فاعلن	tan ta tan	— ∪ —
3.	mafāʿīlun	مفاعيلن	ta tan tan tan	∪ — — —
4.	fāʿilätun	فاعلاتن	tan ta tan tan	— ∪ — —
5.	mustafʿilun	مستفعلن	tan tan ta tan	— — ∪ —
6.	mafʿūlätu	مفعولاتٔ	tan tan tan ta	— — — ∪
7.	faʿilätun	فعلاتن	ta ta tan tan	∪ ∪ — —
8.	mafäʿilun	مفاعلن	ta tan ta tan	∪ — ∪ —
9.	mufäʿalatun	مفاعلتن	ta tan ta ta tan	∪ — ∪ ∪ —
10.	mutafäʿilun	متفاعلن	ta ta tan ta tan	∪ ∪ — ∪ —

The poetic feet are combined to build meters. In Persian poetry the following meters, or bahr, are most typical.[29] Their rhythmic

---

27. See p. 105 for a discussion of rhythm in practice.
28. See Genʾichi Tsuge, "Rhythmic Aspects of the Avaz in Persian Music," Ethnomusicology 14 (May 1970), 205–227, for recent work on rhythm in classical Persian music.
29. Compiled from Parviz Natal Khanlari, Vazn-e Sheir-e Farsi (Tehran, 1958), G. S. Ranking, The Elements of Arabic and Persian Prosody (Bombay, 1885), Adib Sabar Tarmedi (fifteenth century Hejri), Avazn Sheir-e Arabi va Farsi, ed. Mujtaba Minovi (Tehran, n.d.), and Anonymous, Badʿ va ʿAruz va Qafieh (Tehran, Vezarat-e Farhang, 1964).

The Meters of Persian Poetry

Meter	Arabic translation	Mnemonics	Times stated	Rhythmic notation
1. Hazaj	هزج	mafāʿīlun	four	*(musical notation)*
2. Ramal	رمل	fāʿilātun	four	*(musical notation)*
3. Rajaz	رجز	mustafʿilun	four	*(musical notation)*
4. Motaqāreb	متقارب	faʿūlun	four	*(musical notation)*
5. Motdārak	متدارک	faʿlun	four	*(musical notation)*
6. Mazāreh	مضارع	mafāʿ lun fāʿilātun	two	*(musical notation)*
7. Mansareh	منسرح	mustafʿilun mafʿūlātu	two	*(musical notation)*
8. Moqtazab	منقتضب	mafʿūlātu mustafʿilun	two	*(musical notation)*
9. Mujtas	مجتث	mafāʿilun fāʿilātun	two	*(musical notation)*
10. Khafif	خفیف	fāʿilātun mustafʿilun fāʿilātun	one	*(musical notation)*
11. Sariʾ	سریع	mustafʿilun mustafʿilun mafʿūlātu	one	*(musical notation)*
12. Qarīb	قریب	mafāʿ lun mafāʿ lun fāʿilātun	one	*(musical notation)*
13. Moshākel	مشاکل	fāʿ latun mafāʿ lun mafāʿ lun	one	*(musical notation)*

equivalent in musical notation will be given to illustrate how the poetry of any mode could be set to music.[30]

30. See pp. 128–130 for musical examples of verses in the mujtas and ramal meters; see also pp. 138–139 for the use of poetry in performing a dastgah.

3   The Radif of Persian Art Music

Persian art music is based on a large collection of melodies known as the radif (row). Depending on the knowledge of the performer the radif contains anywhere from one to three hundred melodies, or gusheh, organized into seven main systems, dastgah, and five auxiliary systems, naghmeh. For a performance of traditional music, a performer selects a number of gusheh-ha, not from the entire radif, but from one dastgah, to use as a framework for his improvisation. In Persian music the performer has a wide latitude for originality, especially because the number of gusheh-ha in a dastgah, their order, the ways of joining them, and the styles in which each may be played are only loosely defined by tradition.

A central problem in analyzing the radif is this: there is no one authentic version of any melody. This might well be expected, considering that each gusheh functions only as a model for improvisation, not as a finished composition. In a music that is improvised, the major objective is individual expression rather than a strict adherence to the model; and to be judged creative, a performer must alter and embellish the gusheh. Also, the radif has been handed down orally for centuries. Every master had, and to a large extent still has, his own version of each gusheh that is passed on to his students and followers. Notation was not widely used for teaching purposes until the twentieth century, and much of this music is still taught by rote. For these reasons, there is very little consensus among Persian musicians concerning the melodies of the radif.

Illustrating this wide latitude of musical opinion is the recent attempt of the Iranian government to prepare an official version of the radif. Because so many variations exist, even among the musicians of one city, Tehran, it was rightly decided that a compilation of opinion was necessary to ascertain the most authentic reading for each gusheh. A panel of the country's leading musicians was chosen, which was to meet weekly for the length of time necessary to agree upon and prepare this "official radif." Anyone who is familiar with Iran, or with any culture where values of individuality are prized over and above collective thinking and where artistic independence is the chief merit of a musical performance, would recognize that the chances of this group's ever reaching agreement were remarkably slim. Indeed, the panel was soon disbanded, and it was decided that, instead of performing musicians, the country's leading musicologists—supposedly a more scientific, more objective group—should make the choice. Apparently this group achieved even less consensus than the first, for the task was finally given to a single person. Mussa Ma'ruffi did complete a transciption of the radif, which the government of Iran celebrated by a lavish publication. (It is noteworthy that these difficulties are not related in the French translation but only in the Persian version of the preface.) Although that official radif claims to be based on different radif-ha by many leading masters, it is more likely that it is solely the work of the transcriber, Mr. Ma'ruffi. Hence, to present a less biased sample, this study will quote several other versions of each melody in addition to gusheh-ha from the Ma'ruffi radif.

Reliable sources for brief musical illustrations of each dastgah are the theory books. In the Persian language three major works have been written in this century by the musicians responsible for most musical publications in Iran: Hedayat, Vaziri, and Khaleqi.[1] A fourth work containing musical examples from each dastgah, many of them original, was written in German by the Persian theorist Khatchi Khatchi.[2] In a French source by Mehdi Barkechli, the musical examples are taken from a less accessible Persian

1. Mehdi Gholi Hedayat, *Madjma'al Advar* (Tehran, 1938); Ali Naqi Vaziri, *Musiqi-ye Nazari* (Tehran, 1934); Ruhollah Khaleqi, *Nazari be Musiqi*, II (Tehran, 1938).
2. Khatchi Khatchi, *Der Dastgah* (Regensburg, 1962). See also Eckart Wilkens, *Künstler und Amateure im persischen Santurspiel*, Kölner Beiträge zur Musikforschung, Band XLV (Regensburg, 1967).

source.[3] And, an excellent theoretical work in English, containing the largest number of musical illustrations of all the theory books, is the dissertation by Hormoz Farhat.[4]

Collections of typical gusheh-ha from each dastgah are found in instruction manuals, now published for most instruments. The first of these, a landmark in the use of Western notation for Persian music, was published in 1913 in Berlin by Ali Naqi Vaziri.[5] Another, for violin, also by Vaziri, appeared later.[6] And a series of teaching manuals was compiled by Ruhollah Khaleqi for use in his newly founded Conservatory of National Music.[7] Several other teachers in Tehran have also written manuals for their particular instruments. The most widely used publications are the works of Abol Hassan Saba (d. 1957). Three versions of his radif have been published, one for violin, one for santur, and one for tar and sehtar.[8] In contrast to examples from theory books, the pieces in these teaching manuals, especially those in the Saba books, are remarkably close to performance practice. Each of these pieces could be regarded as a finished composition, and they are often performed quite literally by younger musicians.

Of the few transcriptions of the entire radif, that is, those containing several hundred pieces, the first was that of the statesman and amateur musician Mehdi Gholi Hedayat. A former prime minister of Iran and also a student of Mirza Abdullah, Hedayat spent seven years transcribing the radif as played to him by the physician Montazem al-Hokama. This manuscript version of the radif, dated 1928, is now in the library of the Conservatory of National Music.

The radif of Mussa Ma'ruffi, which has official sanction, is also significant for its accessibility. More than one thousand copies

3. "La musique iranienne," in L'histoire de la musique, ed. Roland Manuel, Encyclopédie de la Pléiade, vol. 9 (Paris, 1960), pp. 453–524. The musical examples are taken from among those in Vaziri's Musique-ye Nazari, II, 30–171. The same French article is also used in its entirety in MTI.

4. "The Dastgah Concept in Persian Music" (Ph.D. diss., University of California, Los Angeles, 1965; University Microfilms 66:226).

5. Dastur-e Tar. A second edition was published in Tehran in 1936.

6. Dastur-e Violin (Tehran, 1933).

7. Dastur-e Moqadamati, Tar va Sehtar (Tehran, 1951).

8. See bibliography.

were printed in 1963, and the Ministry of Art and Culture plans several more editions. Having reached the music libraries of many universities in the United States and Europe, this is likely to be the single most influential transcription of the radif for students in Iran and abroad.[9]

A final source, not directly quoted but used as a guide in selecting the examples that follow, is oral tradition as transmitted through live performances. Among the musicians whose performances were used are Ahmad Ebadi, Nur Ali Borumand, Khatereh Parvaneh, Mohammad Heydari, Faromarz Payvar, Kassayi, Hossein Malek, Hushang Zarif, and Banan. Tape recordings and transcriptions prepared by the author and by Gen'ichi Tsuge were also used for this purpose.

The melodies quoted for each dastgah are those of its first gusheh, the daramad. This gusheh, which determines the name as well as much of the character of the entire dastgah, may be considered the single most important melody in the dastgah. The initial gusheh, however, does not represent the dastgah completely, for one important characteristic of each dastgah is its entire system of gusheh-ha. But, within the scope of this present study, it was judged preferable to consider only one gusheh from each dastgah in broader detail, mentioning some of the other gusheh-ha only briefly.[10] For each of the twelve dastgah systems, at least four musical examples will be given to illustrate the daramad, two from the theoretical literature and two from a literature closer to musical practice. The briefest and most explicit musical quotations are from the theory books. Of these, two versions will be presented in order to show variation in

9. Because of the official sponsorship and wide circulation of this volume, many people feel that the Ma'ruffi version may tend to freeze the radif, discouraging further transcriptions. Passed over in the choice of a radif for publication by the Ministry of Culture was that of the violinist Ibrahim Mansuri. His complete radif, notated for violin, is yet unpublished and is known only to a small circle of musicians. A radif as detailed and important as the Ma'ruffi radif is that of Nur Ali Borumand. Although this radif is presently unpublished and hence less widely accessible than that of Mr. Ma'ruffi, it is reputedly an equal or more authentic version of the Abdullah tradition. Mr. Borumand, who teaches in the newly formed music department at the University of Tehran, has also lectured at the University of Illinois, where portions of his radif have been recorded.

10. Abundant musical examples of the important gusheh-ha in each dastgah may be found in Farhat, "The Dastgah Concept." See also Bruno Nettl, *Daramad of Chahargah: A Study in the Performance Practice of Persian Music* (Detroit, 1972).

the melody acceptable even between two musicians as close as master and disciple. The first in each case is by Ali Naqi Vaziri; the second, by his pupil and close associate, Ruhollah Khaleqi. The third example for each dastgah is taken from one of the radif-ha of Abol Hassan Saba, selected because his are the most popular teaching manuals in Tehran today and are close to what is actually performed by contemporary musicians. The fourth example, the one most like an improvised performance in a traditional manner, is that from the Maᶜruffi radif.[11] Finally, for a few dastgah-ha, additional examples of special interest are presented.

According to present usage, each dastgah is normally played on a certain pitch for each instrument. For instance, Shur is most often played in A on the violin, G on the santur, and G on the tar and sehtar. This pitch is called rast kuk (right tuning). When the instrumentalist performs with a singer whose voice is not suited to this pitch, he uses chap kuk (left tuning), which is a perfect fourth lower. But, in order to facilitate comparison between the different versions of each gusheh within a single dastgah and also between different dastgah-ha, all the examples that follow have been transposed to start on the note c′ or c″. The pitch on which this piece was written in the original sources is indicated in brackets. And in the text, the rast kuk for the three most popular instruments will be listed.

The order of presentation of the dastgah-ha is close to that used by many Persian theorists: Shur and its four naghmeh; Mahur; Homayun and its naghmeh; Sehgah; Chahargah; Nava; and Rast Panjgah. This arrangement seems not to be based on any intrinsic feature of the twelve systems but rather on popularity. Shur and its four naghmeh are the ones most often played in Persia today, whereas Nava and Rast Panjgah are hardly played at all. The dastgah-ha in between these seven are equally common, with perhaps a slight preference for Mahur and Esfahan.

Two sets of recordings of Persian art music that could be consulted in conjunction with this chapter are generally accessible in Western music libraries: The Folkways recording *Classical*

---

11. Examples from the Maᶜruffi radif will also be used for the discussion of improvisation in chapter 4.

Music of Iran: Dastgah Systems contains all twelve dastgah and all the important instruments. The Bärenreiter recordings, *A Musical Anthology of the Orient, Iran I and II*, tend to have longer selections, but they contain only Abu Ata, Bayat-e Tork, Dashti, Sehgah, Chahargah, Bakhtiari (in Homayun) and Esfahan.[12]

The radif is a body of material that has been handed down mainly by oral tradition, and there is no one certified version of any part of it. Furthermore, there is no single theoretical opinion agreed to by all Persian musicians. Hence, the examples of the daramad-ha quoted in score below and the listing of the important gusheh-ha given in the text are by no means exclusive. They were presented as objectively as possible, but by a foreigner whose knowledge of the tradition is necessarily limited. Moreover, these examples stem from one tradition, the radif of Mirza Abdullah as transmitted mainly through Mussa Maᶜruffi, Abol Hassan Saba, and Nur Ali Borumand. This school does not represent the entire maqam tradition in Iran but merely one of its major branches.[13] Native Persian readers and non-Persians who have learned the radif from a different source may well disagree with these selections and interpretations.

THE DASTGAH SHUR

That this dastgah heads the list of the twelve systems in most writings is indeed appropriate. Not only is Shur the dastgah with by far the greatest number of gusheh-ha, but it is also the most popular one. Shur might even by considered as a kind of basic Persian mode since it is parent to four secondary dastgah and is related through modulatory gusheh-ha to several more. The name *Shur* reflects its popularity, for it means "spicy" or "clever."[14]

12. Folkways FW 8831 and 8832; Bärenreiter-Musicaphon, UNESCO Collection, BM 30 L 2004 and 2005.

13. For this suggestion I am very grateful to Bruno Nettl.

14. Three studies of this dastgah are: Khatchi Khatchi, "Das Intervallbildungsprinzip des persischen Dastgah Shur," *Jahrbuch für musikalische Volks- und Völkerkünde* 3 (1967), pp. 70–84; Edith Gerson-Kiwi, *The Persian Doctrine of Dastga-Composition* (Tel-Aviv, 1963); Mohammad Taghi Massoudieh, *Awaz-e Sur: Zur Melodiebildung in der persischen Kunstmusik* (Regensburg, 1968).

The scale of Shur is similar either to the Western natural minor scale with the second degree lowered by a quarter tone or to the phrygian mode with the second degree raised by a quarter tone: C D♭ E♭ F G A♭ B♭ C. Both the shahed and ist are the first note, C. The moteghayer is the fifth note, which is lowered to G-koron for the gusheh of Shahnaz. The note on which the daramad starts is frequently the seventh scale step, B-flat.

Because Shur is so popular, there are several acceptable versions of the daramad. The most usual is the one given in Examples 7–11. These melodies feature an ascent to the fourth scale degree and a slower, more ornamental, descent. The second degree, D-koron, which forms a neutral second with the tonic, is particularly stressed in all examples. Another version of the daramad of Shur, shown in Example 12, descends a fifth rather than ascending a fourth.

Some of the important gusheh-ha of Shur are Shahnaz, Salmak, Gereyli, and Razavi on the fourth scale degree, and Bozorg and Hosseini on the eighth. The rast kuk for Shur is: G or A for the tar and sehtar, G for the santur, and A for the violin.

According to Khaleqi, the dastgah of Shur contains so many nuances that its character cannot be defined simply and will differ considerably according to the listener. In Khaleqi's opinion, Shur has an association of seriousness, as do most of the Persian dastgah-ha. He says that Shur is a counselor, one who gives moral teaching. The voice of Shur is noble, mystic, and near to the spirit of the Iranian people. It is an older person speaking—not like Dashti, who is a youth who cannot control his sadness and cries easily. When hearing Shur we see lovely scenery— gardens, flowers, rivers. Hearing this causes us to be silent in order to appreciate the silence of nature. The sentiment of Shur is one appreciated by Oriental people.[15]

SHUR

EXAMPLE 7.   Vaziri, *MN*, p. 30. (e′)

---

15. From a conversation with Mr. Khaleqi. Similar ideas may be found in his *Nazari be Musiqi*, p. 131.

EXAMPLE 8.   Khaleqi, *NM*, p. 132. (a′)

EXAMPLE 9.   Maᶜruffi, *MTI*, p. 1 (g)

EXAMPLE 10.   Saba, *DAV*, p. 21. (e″)

EXAMPLE 11.   The daramad of Shur

EXAMPLE 12.   Another version of the daramad

EXAMPLE 13.   The daramad of Shur, Borumand (Tsuge transcription). (g′)

THE NAGHMEH-HA OF SHUR

Attached to the dastgah of Shur are four auxiliary dastgah called naghmeh (melody). It is likely that these satellites of Shur—Abu Ata, Afshari, Bayat-e Tork, and Dashti—were originally melodies among the gusheh-ha of Shur. Then, because they were well liked, perhaps in a certain region of the country, they were elaborated, and secondary melodies were added to them until they achieved their present semi-independent status. Dashti seems to have come from the region of Dashtestan. Tork and Afshari are names of groups of people, the Turks and the tribe of Afshari. Abu Ata, meaning "father of Ata," also has an ethnographic name, Dastan-e Arab, "tale of the Arab."

The five naghmeh differ from the seven dastgah in having a smaller repertory and a narrower range in their basic melodies. In addition, they are more or less dependent on their parent dastgah.[16] The closeness with which Shur's four naghmeh are

16. The four naghmeh of Shur are also called mote'aleqat'e Shur, meaning "dependents of Shur."

attached to it varies with each one. All share one characteristic with their parent dastgah—a similar feeling or ethos. To describe this characteristic, Vaziri likens a naghmeh to a provincial city. In Iran, where each province tends to be distinctive, a city in any one province has the general flavor of that province, a flavor different from any other. Carrying this over to music, he states that, "just as the city of Meshed has the general hue of the province of Khorassan, Bayat-e Tork has the same hue as Shur."[17]

The naghmeh-ha are also related to Shur in a more specific sense. At the close of a performance of a naghmeh, or even as early as the closing of the daramad, the naghmeh often resolves to its parent dastgah. Abu Ata is most dependent in this way since, by tradition, it always ends in Shur. Dashti usually does, also. Bayat-e Tork may or may not, depending upon the wishes of the performer. And Afshari seldom ends in Shur except when the gusheh of Rahavi is played.

A most important element defining each naghmeh is the position of its ist and shahed on the Shur scale. The positions of the naghmeh-ha of Shur may be tabulated as follows:

	Abu Ata	Afshari	Bayat-e Tork	Dashti
Ist (stopping note)	2	2	3	3 (or 5)
Shahed (note of stress)	4	4	3	5

The positions of the four naghmeh are also shown in Example 14.

Examples 15–22 of the daramad-ha from each naghmeh have been transposed to the Shur scale on c′ in order to illustrate the relationship to the parent dastgah of Shur.

EXAMPLE 14.

17. *Musiqi-ye Nazari*, p. 20.

ABU ATA

EXAMPLE 15.

EXAMPLE 16. Khaleqi, *NM*, p. 136. (b-flat′)

AFSHARI

EXAMPLE 17.

EXAMPLE 18. Vaziri, *MN*, p. 43. (a′)

BAYAT-E TORK

EXAMPLE 19.

EXAMPLE 20. Khaleqi, *NM*, p. 140. (c″)

DASHTI

EXAMPLE 21.

EXAMPLE 22.   Vaziri, *MN*, p. 45. (g′)

THE NAGHMEH ABU ATA

Abu Ata (father of Ata) is the naghmeh most closely associated with the parent dastgah of Shur. It is customary to write the same scale for Abu Ata as for Shur, C Dᵖ Eᵇ F G Aᵇ Bᵇ C, mentioning that the note of stress, shahed, is the fourth degree, and the note of stopping, ist, is the second. When the scale is transposed to C for the examples below, the result is notationally awkward: C Dᵖ Eᵖ F♯ Gᵖ Aᵖ Bᵖ C (the formidable interval between the fourth and fifth scale degrees is merely a half step). In either configuration, the initial fourth is not perfect, an unusual feature of this system. Perhaps this causes the range of its daramad to be narrow—a third rather than a fourth.

The initial daramad of Abu Ata features a rapid ascent of a neutral third, C to E-koron and an immediate descent, repeated with increasing elaboration. The melody always returns to Shur, one degree below Abu Ata's ist, for the final cadence. (See Examples 23–26.)

The most important gusheh of Abu Ata is Hejaz, on the fourth degree (which is the fifth degree of Shur). This name relates to the alternate name of this naghmeh, Dastan-e Arab, for the Hejaz is that province in Arabia famous for containing Medina and Mecca, birthplaces of Islam. Also starting on the fourth degree of Abu Ata is an unusual measured gusheh with a characteristic opening leap of a fifth, Chahar Bagh (four gardens). The usual pitch for Abu Ata is D for tar and sehtar, G for santur, and A for violin.

ABU ATA

EXAMPLE 23.   Khaleqi, *NM*, p. 132. (b-flat′)

EXAMPLE 24.   Vaziri, *MN*, p. 36. (f′)

EXAMPLE 25.   Ma᷄ruffi, *MTI*, p. 1. (e-flat′)

EXAMPLE 26.   Saba, *DAV*, p. 8. (f′)

THE NAGHMEH AFSHARI

This auxiliary dastgah bears the name of one of the larger tribes in Iran. In the scale of Shur, Afshari stresses the fourth degree, as does Abu Ata, but the two naghmeh are quite different in character. Abu Ata starts on the second degree of Shur and rises to the fourth, whereas Afshari opens on the fourth degree, stresses it heavily, and then descends. (See Examples 27–30.) Another difference is that Afshari has a changing tone, or moteghayer, on the fifth degree of Shur, which may have two values differing by a quarter tone.[18] Afshari is the naghmeh most independent of the parent dastgah, for a performance of Afshari rarely ends in Shur.

Three scale degrees of Shur are prominent in the daramad of Afshari: the second, which is the ist of Afshari; the fourth, which is the shahed; and the seventh, a decorating tone. Persian theorists write the scale of Afshari from the seventh degree of Shur: Bᵇ C Dᵖ Eᵇ F G Aᵇ Bᵇ, or, transposed, C D Eᵖ F G A Bᵇ C. This transcription gives a scale with fewer accidentals than the one obtained when Afshari is transposed from its note of stopping, D-koron: Dᵖ Eᵇ F G Aᵇ Bᵇ C Dᵖ, or, transposed, C Dᵖ Eᵖ F♯

---

18. The examples do not use the moteghayer, but it can be observed in the Maᶜruffi radif by glancing through the first eleven pieces in Afshari, where the note A alternates between A-natural and A–koron.

G♭ A♭ B♭ C. For the sake of consistency with the other examples in this study, however, the latter is used in the musical examples.

The most important gusheh-ha belonging to Afshari are Araq (Iraq) and Rohab, both on the sixth degree. The rast kuk for Afshari is C for tar and sehtar, F for santur, and B-koron for violin.

AFSHARI

EXAMPLE 27.   Vaziri, *MN*, p. 43. (a′)

EXAMPLE 28.   Khaleqi, *NM*, p. 147. (b-flat′)

EXAMPLE 29.   Ma'ruffi, *MTI*, p. 1. (e-flat′)

EXAMPLE 30.   Saba, *DDV*, p. 16. (b-flat′)

THE NAGHMEH BAYAT-E TORK

Bayat-e Tork (verses of the Turk, or verses of beauty) has another appellation, Bayat-e Zand, which refers to the family of an unusually well regarded eighteenth-century monarch, Karim Khan Zand.

The scale of Bayat-e Tork is customarily written from the third degree of Shur: E♭ F G A♭ B♭ C D♭ E♭, or, transposed to C, C D E F G A B♭ C.

Although there is little consensus among the theorists regarding this naghmeh, all seem to agree on one characteristic—the unusual persistence of the shahed, which causes Bayat-e Tork to be a bit monotonous. Example 33 shows this most clearly. To relieve the tonal monotony, some musicians use the fifth degree of Bayat-e Tork as the note of cadencing. (See Examples 31–34.)

Two of the important gusheh-ha of Bayat-e Tork happen to be taken from the dastgah of Mahur: Shekasteh and Delkash, both on the fifth scale degree. Qatar, a Kurdish melody, is played on the first degree. The rast kuk is F for tar and sehtar, B-flat for santur, and C for violin.

BAYAT-E TORK

EXAMPLE 31.   Vaziri, *MN*, p. 39. (g′)

EXAMPLE 32.   Khaleqi, *NM*, p. 140. (c″)

EXAMPLE 33.   Maꜥruffi, *MTI*, p. 1. (f′)

EXAMPLE 34.   Saba, *DDV*, p. 21. (c″)

THE NAGHMEH DASHTI

This naghmeh, clearly the most important of the auxiliary dastgah-ha belonging to Shur, is also more closely related to Iranian folk music than any other dastgah or naghmeh of Persian art music. Many folk melodies are included among the gusheh of Dashti: Gilaki, Dashtestani, Bayat-e Kord, and Chupani (a shepherd), to name a few. Moreover, it is generally felt that a large percentage of the folk music heard in Iran has the same "feeling" as Dashti and may even have a similar scale and melodic shape. In fact, Barkechli states that Dashti is the basis of musical folklore in the northern provinces.[19] The name, however, comes from the region of Dashtestan in the south.

Theorists usually write the Shur scale for Dashti with the third degree as ist and the fifth as shahed. Transposed to C, the Dashti scale is the same as that of Bayat-e Tork: C D E F G A B♭ C.

For the daramad of Dashti there is unusual consensus in the sources. All transposed versions start on C, the ist, and rise to stress the shahed E. Even the rhythmic figure at the opening is the same for three of the four examples. A second rise goes as high as the fifth. At the close is a long descent, not back to the C, but down another third to the ist of the parent dastgah Shur. The Saba version is noteworthy since it rearranges the melody somewhat while preserving these essential features. To stress the final descent, the shahed is lowered by a quarter tone in all versions. It is thus a moteghayer. Note that this change necessitates a change of register in Example 38, which is for santur. (See Examples 35–38.)

In another frequently played version of the melody of Dashti, the opening contains a prominent rise of a fifth from the ist of Shur to the shahed of Dashti. (In this transposition of Dashti the ist of Shur is a, and the fifth is a to e'.) A simple melodic outline for this version is shown in Example 39, but a more customary

19. *MTI*, p. 43.

opening is a leap of a fifth, rather than a filled-in interval, as shown by the melody of Example 40.

The most important gusheh in Dashti is Oshaq (lovers) on the upper sixth degree. This degree is also an octave above the ist of Shur. For the gusheh of Oshaq, the fifth degree of Dashti is lowered by a quarter tone. Rast kuk for Dashti is F for tar and sehtar, B-flat for santur, and C for violin.

The melodic shape of Dashti is well illustrated by one of the composed forms of Persian music outside of the radif, the tasnif. In the transposition used in Example 41, the ist of Shur is b, that of Dashti is d' and its shahed is f♯'. The opening measures show the leap of the fifth from the ist of Shur to the shahed or third of Dashti. The changing of this note by a quarter-tone inflection appears in measure 5, where the f-sharp becomes f-sori. In measure 30, the leap up to b' indicates a movement toward the gusheh of Oshaq, but the melody returns immediately to Dashti and closes in Shur.

DASHTI

EXAMPLE 35.   Vaziri, *MN*, p. 45. (g')

EXAMPLE 36.   Khaleqi, *NM*, p. 151. (c″)

EXAMPLE 37.   Maʿruffi, *MTI*, p. 1. (f')

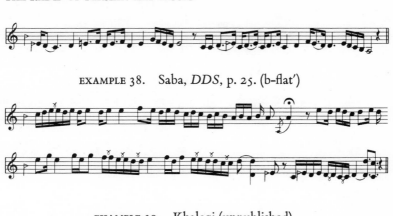

EXAMPLE 38. Saba, *DDS*, p. 25. (b-flat')

EXAMPLE 39. Khaleqi (unpublished)

EXAMPLE 40. Khaleqi (unpublished)

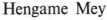

EXAMPLE 41. Abol Hassem Aref, 1908

Hengame Mey

Hen - ga - me me - yo........   fas - le go - lo gash - te....

... ja - nam gash - te......   Kho - da gash - te..

cha - man..... shod..... Dar - ba - re ba - ha......, ri

to - hi az za - - gho..... ja - nam za - - gho...

... kho - da za - gho za - ghan....... shod......
... az ab - re ka - ra - m khe - te - ye rey
rash - ke kho - tan shod....... del - tan - go -
cho man mor - ghe..... ja - nam mar - ghe -
- gha - fass bah - re va - tan....... shod.
che.. kaj... raf - ta... ri ey........ charkh,
sa - re... kin da - ri ey..... charkh,
na din da - ri na a........ in da -
ri na a... in da - ri ey....... charkh. *D.C.*

THE DASTGAH MAHUR

This dastgah is especially distinct from the other eleven systems in an important characteristic—its ethos. Mahur expresses "l'audace, la gaité, l'optimisme,"[20] feelings quite distinct from those of most of the other dastgah-ha, which are closer to the

20. Barkechli, *MTI*, p. 45.

pessimistic end of the emotional spectrum. This characteristic of Mahur might well be attributed to its scale, which is, in essence, the same as the plagal form of the Western major, a scale generally felt to express brighter emotions. The name *Mahur* even seems close to "major," although its meaning, "rising ground," is not related.

Like Shur, Mahur is one of the more popular dastgah-ha in use today. For this reason, there are several acceptable versions of the basic melody. The one presented in Examples 42–45 is the most widely recognized melody. It starts on the ist, here c″, descends to the dominant and then rises to the supertonic, often continuing to the upper dominant before descending to the ist. That both the dominant and supertonic are important scale degrees is demonstrated by the expanded version of the daramad, Example 44. The note of stress, shahed, is debated among theorists. Some claim the tonic, others the dominant. In either case, the strength of a V–I relationship is significant.

All sources concur on the gusheh-ha of Mahur. Most important is the melody on the dominant called *Delkash* (fascinating, winsome), which is a particularly clear example of the kind of modulation that occurs in Persian music. This gusheh adds two accidentals: a koron on the sixth degree and a flat on the seventh: C D E F G A^r B^b C. The tetrachord of Delkash is thus identical to that of the most popular Persian melody type, Shur. A listener who had not heard the opening of a performance of Mahur might think that Delkash was, in fact, Shur. But the melodic contour of this melody and its eventual return to the tonic of Mahur would indicate that it was Delkash.

Another gusheh of Mahur, also on the fifth scale degree, is Shekasteh (broken, or doleful). On the upper tonic are the two gusheh of Araq and Rak. The rast kuk for Mahur is C for tar and sehtar, F for santur, and G for violin.

MAHUR

EXAMPLE 42.   Vaziri, *MN*, p. 70. (c″)

EXAMPLE 43.   Khaleqi, *NM*, p. 167. (d″)

EXAMPLE 44.   Maᶜruffi, *MTI*, p. 5. (c′)

EXAMPLE 45.   Saba, *DDV*, p. 53. (g′)

THE DASTGAH HOMAYUN

The word *Homayun*, meaning "auspicious" or "fortunate," is frequently used as either a first or last name in Iran. Hence, it is likely that the dastgah was named after the musician who composed the chief melody.

The scale of Homayun contains a neutral second and major third in the lower tetrachord and a minor second and minor third in the higher: C D^p E F G A$^\flat$ B$^\flat$ C. Thus, it can be regarded as a major form of Shur, since Shur has the same scale but with a minor third in the lower tetrachord: C D^p E$^\flat$ F G A$^\flat$ B$^\flat$ C. The lower tetrachord of Homayun is also identical to that of Chahargah.

The daramad of Homayun in Examples 46–49 is characterized by a stepwise ascent to the second scale degree from the lower sixth. This second degree is the shahed for the daramad. In most versions the ist is not the tonic but the seventh.[21] Thus the tonic is unimportant at first. It comes into prominence later in the composition with those cadence formulae called forud (descent), which are played between some of the gusheh-ha to reinforce the tonic. The tonic is also the note that ends the dastgah.

The most important gusheh-ha in contemporary usage are Bidad on the fifth degree, Oshaq on the upper tonic, and on the fourth degree, Shushtari and the song of the renowned Persian lovers Leyla and Majnun, the Romeo and Juliet of Iran. The rast kuk of Homayun is G for tar and sehtar, G for santur, and A for violin.

HOMAYUN

EXAMPLE 46.   Vaziri, *MN*, p. 96. (g′)

EXAMPLE 47.   Khaleqi, *NM*, p. 182. (a′)

EXAMPLE 48.   Ma‘ruffi, *MTI*, pp. 1–2. (g′)

21. In the Ma‘ruffi radif, however, it is the tonic.

EXAMPLE 49.   Saba, *DSS*, p. 7. (g′)

THE NAGHMEH ESFAHAN (BAYAT-E ESFAHAN)

Esfahan, capital of Iran during the brilliant Safavid period (sixteenth through eighteenth centuries), is architecturally the most beautiful city in Iran, and the saying "Esfahan nesfe Jehan ast" (Esfahan is half the world), recalls its splendor. The name *Esfahan* is found in lists of dastgah-ha used during the medieval period in Iran. Surprisingly, the scale is not too dissimilar from that used today. As given by the thirteenth-century theorist Safi al-Din, it is C D Eᵇ F G Aᵖ Bᵇ B♮ C.[22]

The present scale of Esfahan, derived from the fourth degree of its parent dastgah, Homayun, is F G Aᵇ Bᵇ C Dᵖ E F, or, C D Eᵇ F G Aᵖ B C, a harmonic minor scale with the sixth degree

22. D'Erlanger, *MA*, III, 381–382.

raised a quarter tone. Contemporary Persian music, especially the popular and semiclassical varieties, often uses the Western minor scale for pieces written in Esfahan instead of the authentic Esfahan scale.[23]

The daramad of Esfahan, Examples 50–53, usually contains an upward leap of a fourth to the tonic, followed by a descent. The shahed is clearly the fourth degree, but theorists disagree on which note is the ist. Vaziri and Khaleqi say it is the sixth, and two of the four examples do indeed cadence on this note. But equally often, the lower tonic, c′, functions as the note of stopping.

That Esfahan is now designated as a naghmeh is a change from the radif tradition earlier in the twentieth century. In the earliest record of Mirza Abdullah's radif, that given by Hedayat, Esfahan is merely one of the thirty-odd gusheh-ha of Homayun.[24] Gradually, it has become more independent, until, in current usage, it has nearly achieved the full status of a dastgah. Only its small repertory and its frequent return to the tonic of Homayun keeps it in the postion of a naghmeh.

Important gusheh-ha of Esfahan are Bayat-e Rajeh on the second scale degree, and Oshaq on the fifth. The latter gusheh is similar to the gusheh Oshaq in Dashti and Homayun. Rast tuning for Esfahan is D for tar and sehtar, C for santur and D for violin.

ESFAHAN

EXAMPLE 50.   Vaziri, *MN*, p. 163. (d″)

EXAMPLE 51.   Khaleqi, *NM*, p. 189. (d″)

23. Khaleqi states that the raised seventh is also a recent innovation. Esfahan formerly had a lowered seventh, which some musicians still preserve.

24. Khatchi, *Der Dastgah*, p. 22.

EXAMPLE 52.   Maʿruffi, *MTI*, p. 1. (g′)

EXAMPLE 53.   Saba, *DSS*, p. 21. (c″)

THE DASTGAH SEHGAH

Literally, the word *sehgah* means "third place": *seh* is the Persian for "three"; *gah*, the word for "time" or "place." This kind of designation was formerly used both in Persia and in the Arab countries to indicate the degrees of the scale. Yek (one) gah was the first degree; do (two) gah, the second; and, similarly, sehgah, chahargah, panjgah, shishgah and haftgah, the third, fourth, fifth, sixth, and seventh degrees.[25] In the early twentieth century, four of these titles were still used in Persia. Huart reports that yekgah was used for the first degree of the scale, dogah for the fifth, sehgah for the sixth degree flattened by a quarter tone, and chahargah for the seventh flattened by a quarter tone.[26] By

25. D'Erlanger, *MA*, V, 12.
26. *LavE*, p. 3069. See also Nettl, *Daramad of Chahargah*.

the middle of the twentieth century, the French solfege syllables were common in Iran and most of the Middle East. But the Persian gah system survives in the names of several Arabian melody types and three Persian ones, namely, Sehgah, Chahargah, and Rast Panjgah. In contemporary practice these three systems, are further related by sharing certain gusheh-ha, for example Zabol, Zanguleh, and Zang-e Shotor.

The scale of Sehgah is problematical. When written from the note that is both shahed and ist, here c′, the scale is C D♭ E♭ F G♭ A♭ B♭ C. But the fact that this scale has an imperfect fifth is bothersome to some Persian theorists, who feel that scales ought to have perfect fifths. Also, writing the scale this way obscures one of the more important relationships in the dastgah, the stressing of the neutral third below the tonic. Both of these faults are corrected if the scale is written with the shahed as the third note, which is the version given by most theorists: C D E♭ F G A♭ B♭ C. But to be consistent with the other transpositions in this chapter, the first scale, starting from shahed as the tonic, is used in the following examples.

Characteristic of the daramad, and of the Saba melody, which is not, strictly speaking, a daramad but uses the same melody, is a stressing of the tonic, sometimes preceded by the lower third. (See Examples 54–57.) There is a rise to the third, a stressing of it by its neighbor tones, and then a descent to the tonic with the very typical lower third Sehgah cadence.

The most important gusheh-ha of Sehgah are Zabol on the third scale degree, Muyeh on the fourth, and Mokhalef on the sixth. Rast kuk for Sehgah is E-koron for tar and sehtar, A-koron for santur, and B-koron for violin.

SEHGAH

EXAMPLE 54.   Vaziri, *MN*, p. 142. (e-koron′)

EXAMPLE 55.   Khaleqi, *NM*, p. 203. (b-koron′)

EXAMPLE 56.   Ma'ruffi, *MTI*, p. 1. (g')

EXAMPLE 57.   Saba, *DAS*, p. 21. (a')

THE DASTGAH CHAHARGAH

Chahargah (fourth place) is one numeral higher than Sehgah. Although these two dastgah are related in name as well as through several of their gusheh-ha, their scales are quite dissimilar. The distinctive scale of Chahargah contains two identical tetrachords, C D♭ E F and G A♭ B C, each containing a neutral second and a major third. There are also two intervals close to augmented seconds, D♭ to E and A♭ to B, not often found in Persian music.[27]

27. Hormoz Farhat has devoted considerable attention to these intervals in "The Augmented Second Interval and Its Use in Persian Music," *Musik-e Iran*, 1343, #1. The augmented second is also found in Homayun.

For the chief melody of Chahargah, one finds general agreement in nearly all sources—a rare occurrence in even this particular dastgah tradition. (See Examples 58–62.) The melodic motive that identifies Chahargah is the rising neutral third to the tonic, A-koron to C. This motive is stressed at the opening and again at the cadence. The A-koron receives additional emphasis by a trill from the note below. The trill of a neutral second and a stressing of the neutral third gives a particular sound to Chahargah, making it one of the most easily recognizable dastgah-ha.

Aside from the motives used for opening and closing of the daramad, the material between is also quite similar in all the sources. Immediately after the characteristic opening, there is a quick descent back to the A-koron, followed by a slower, more elaborate rise, which exceeds the tonic by a major third and then returns to it. In this unusually well defined melody, there is even some rhythmic similarity in all versions of the opening and closing sections. The middle sections in all versions are in an even rhythm of sixteenth notes with quarter or half notes used to emphasize the important degrees of the tetrachord.

Of the gusheh-ha belonging to Chahargah, the most important are Muyeh on the third degree, Zabol on the fourth, Hesar on the fifth (with the fourth degree raised to provide a leading tone), and Mokhalef on the sixth. These gusheh-ha correspond to the most important gusheh-ha of Sehgah in their names, in the scale degrees they stress, and, less exactly, in their melodies.

Chahargah, like Mahur, is one of the happier dastgah-ha of Persian music. Evidence for its joyous character is the popular wedding piece in Example 62. Rast kuk for Chahargah is C for tar and sehtar, C for santur, and D for violin.

CHAHARGAH

EXAMPLE 58.   Vaziri, *MN*, p. 121. (c″)

EXAMPLE 59.   Khaleqi, *NM*, p. 220. (d″)

EXAMPLE 60.   Maᶜruffi, *MTI*, p. 1. (c′)

EXAMPLE 61.   Saba, *DDV*, p. 46. (d″)

EXAMPLE 62.   A Wedding Piece in Chahargah (Khaleqi transcription)

Refrain: Ey-yar mo-ba-rak   ba-da.

THE DASTGAH NAVA

The last two dastgah systems are rather special as evidence of a process of evolution in the radif, for of all twelve systems, Nava and Rast Panjgah are least popular and are seldom performed today. That they both have large repertories, are not now connected to any other systems, and were firmly established in the early versions of the radif by both Hedayat and Nasir, suggests that these dastgah are in the process of leaving the radif rather than entering it.[28] One reason for their unpopularity might be their similarity to two of the most popular dastgah systems: Nava is similar to the dastgah of Shur, starting on its fifth degree; and Rast Panjgah is similar to Mahur. Because many present-day musicians are no longer especially interested in an extensive knowledge of the radif, they would be more likely to perform Shur and Mahur, which are extremely well known, than to go to the trouble of learning new repertory.[29]

The scale of Nava (tune, or air) is like a natural minor scale with a slightly raised sixth degree or half-flat: C D E♭ F G A♭ B♭ C. It bears a strong relation to the scale of Shur, as both tetrachords have the same configuration only their position is reversed, that is, Shur's tonic is Nava's dominant.

The daramad of Nava does not have a clear profile in Examples 63–66. Characteristics that appear in each, although not in the same order, are a stressing of the tonic, C, and a descent to the shahed, A. Vaziri goes so far as to end on this A. Three examples end with the cadence figure f″–f″–c″ (IV–I), called Bal-e Kabutar ("wings of the dove"). Although this figure is also found in other dastgah-ha, it is particularly characteristic of Nava.

Important gusheh-ha of Nava are Gavesht on the second degree and Nahoft on the fifth. Rast tuning is G for tar and sehtar, C for santur, and A for violin.

---

28. Khatchi, Der Dastgah, pp. 17 and 23.

29. In preparing the Folkways recording, I had great trouble obtaining performances of these two dastgah. After failing to obtain tapes from the large collection at the radio station, I finally persuaded a young performer to prepare the performances that now appear. Knowledgeable listeners will recognize that they are very close to the published Saba versions of these two dastgah, suggesting that the performer had not played Nava and Rast Panjgah frequently enough to develop his own improvisatory versions.

NAVA

EXAMPLE 63.   Vaziri, *MN*, pp. 149–150. (g′)

EXAMPLE 64.   Khaleqi, *NM*, p. 156. (g″)

EXAMPLE 65.   Maʿruffi, *MTI*, p. 1. (g′)

EXAMPLE 66.   Saba, *DCS*, pp. 31–32. (c′)

THE DASTGAH RAST PANJGAH

The name of this system has the same derivation as those of two other dastgah-ha, Sehgah and Chahargah. Panjgah indicates the "fifth place." Rast, which in Persian means "right" or "true," could have a number of interpretations. The most likely is that the name refers to the rast system of tuning, as opposed to chap, a tuning one fourth lower. Another possibility is that of two versions of Panjgah, Rast Panjgah is the true or correct version. Finally, the appellation *Rast* might refer to the medieval Arabian melody type of that name.

The scale of Rast Panjgah is identical with that of Mahur, that is, the Western major scale. Evidence of the weakness of the tradition is the scarcity of musical examples of the daramad. Khaleqi gives only the direction to "consult Vaziri."[30] Vaziri, however, does not give the daramad but instead gives the cadence formula, forud. This and the two examples closer to practice, by Ma'ruffi and Saba, show some degree of consensus. (See Examples 68–70.) According to what musicians did tell me about this dastgah, the strongest motive is the figure in Example 67 called *parvaneh* (butterfly).

After the opening daramad, it is common practice to modulate to other dastgah-ha. In itself, this practice seems to indicate the weak knowledge of the special repertory of Rast Panjgah. Another speculation offered by Hormoz Farhat is that Rast Panjgah is thought to have been a student piece used to demonstrate the

---

30. *Nazari be Musiqi*, p. 171.

melodic characteristics of each dastgah in the radif.[31] Rast tuning is F for tar and sehtar, F for santur, and A for violin.

RAST PANJGAH

EXAMPLE 67.   Typical cadence figure

EXAMPLE 68.   Vaziri, *MN*, p. 166. (f′)

EXAMPLE 69.   Maᶜruffi, *MTI*, p. 1. (f′)

EXAMPLE 70.   Saba, *DCS*, pp. 48–49. (f′)

31. This suggestion was made in conversation.

4   The Practice of Persian Art Music: Improvisation

The repertory of melodies that forms the basis of traditional Persian art music is not in itself Persian music, for what is actually played is one step beyond the radif. The individual pieces, gusheh-ha, are not performed literally according to any of the versions given above. Each gusheh is merely a framework. A good performer is expected to fill in the framework, or to elaborate upon the melodic material of the radif, and to do this extemporaneously. Thus, between the radif and a performance is a set of processes forming a separate layer of music theory, which may be designated the "theory of practice." Its counterpart in Western music would be included in composition, but since the composition of Persian music is extemporaneous, this subject may best be labeled "improvisation."

Iranian musicians do not isolate this branch of theory, and they do not teach it formally. In fact, in the literature improvisation is hardly mentioned except for some of the more practical problems, such as realization of the ornaments from Western notation. Indeed, most of the theory of practice comes to an Iranian intuitively. Because music in Iran is still mainly taught by rote (with the aid of printed instruction books), the student simply absorbs the compositional procedures without being aware of them as such. For this reason, a musician is often unable to explain precisely what he is doing during his improvisation. Likewise, Persian music theorists, considering this aspect of music to be an intuitive procedure, do not discuss it in their writings. Therefore, in contrast to the branches of Persian music theory that have been well developed and extensively discussed (the size of the microintervals, for instance), the foreign musicologist has little indigenous methodology or terminology on which to base a study of improvisation.

A further obstacle in this area is the readily apparent discrepancy between the theory of practice and the practice of practice. Not infrequently, after a lengthy interview regarding performance practices, a performer will illustrate the aspects of practice he has just described by playing something entirely different from what he has just said ought to be played. One must realize from the beginning that in Persian music there is no "always," for no rule or custom is inviolable. It is highly unrealistic, therefore, to make any statement about practice without qualifying it with terms such as "generally," "usually," "the typical," or "frequently."

The study of improvisation attempts to get beneath what is intuitive or natural in the musician's performance and by generalizing from many performances, to discover the ordering principles of the performance. For this purpose, the extemporaneous composition of Persian music may be analyzed as a series of decisions. After deciding on the dastgah he will play, the performer must decide which gusheh-ha of that dastgah he will perform, and in what order he will play them. Then there are numerous decisions relating to how each gusheh is to be composed. These include the elaboration and extension of the basic model to create a piece and the joining of several pieces to form that movement of the dastgah performance called the gusheh.

CHOICE OF THE DASTGAH AND ITS GUSHEH-HA

Selection of a dastgah was once dependent upon the time of day, each dastgah, or, even each gusheh, being considered appropriate for a certain hour, like the Indian raga. How strictly this tradition was followed is unknown, as is the period when the practice fell into disuse.[1] It was described as late as the twentieth century

1. Al-Ladhiqi (d. 1494), in his treatise *Risalat al Fathigay fi'l Musiqi*, attributes this

by Mirza Nasir Forsat-e Dowleh in *Bohur el Alhan*,[2] but as a fading historical practice rather than a contemporary one. Presently, the time of day has no relation to the choice of dastgah, as the performer simply selects a dastgah he particularly favors or one that suits his feeling of the moment.[3] When playing for television or radio, a performer may be asked to perform a certain dastgah; or, if the composition includes a tasnif, the dastgah of the tasnif will be used as well for the improvisatory sections from the radif (each tasnif is associated with one particular dastgah). With the exceptions of the two dastgah Nava and Rast Panjgah, used only rarely today, most artists can perform the dastgah equally well and upon request.

When a musician selects a particular dastgah he calls to mind a large repertory of gusheh-ha. He must decide how many to play and in what order. The first of these decisions is naturally dependent on the extent of his knowledge of the radif and on the length of the performance. In an informal music session, the time is virtually unlimited, and, theoretically, the entire repertory of the dastgah might be played. But for a radio or television program, where the performance is generally limited to ten or fifteen minutes at the most, or for the small 45 rpm phonograph recordings common in Iran, the musician performs only the three or four most important gusheh of that dastgah and several

---

practice to al-Farabi and lists the following maqamat with their times of performance (d'Erlanger, *MA*, IV, 455):

Rahavi	at the false sunrise
Husayni	at the true sunrise
Rast	when the sun appears above the horizon
Abu Salik	before noon
Zanguleh	at noon
Ussaq	at afternoon prayers
Hijazi	between afternoon prayers
Isfahan	at sunset
Nawa	at evening prayers
Buzurg	after dinner prayers
Zirafkand	when going to bed

2. Shiraz, 1903, p. 23.

3. The concept of a definite feeling associated with each dastgah—ethos—is also no longer discernible in contemporary music. It was, of course, an essential part of medieval musical speculation. Today different players associate different moods with certain pieces of the radif, but there is little consensus among them as to which feeling is appropriate to which melody. The custom of playing only certain kinds of pieces for certain audiences is set forth in the treatise *Bahjat al Ruh*. This description, along with other unusual instructions for musicians, is contained in Appendix B.

pieces, or tekke-ha.[4] The radif-ha of Mussa Maᶜruffi, Ibrahim
Mansuri, and Mehdi Gholi Hedayat contain an unusually large
number of gusheh-ha for each dastgah. But few of the musicians
performing today know this many, as the practice of learning
the full radif is weakening among the present generation of music
students, who learn a smaller repertory, usually the one in the
Saba instruction manuals. Rather than studying the more obscure
gusheh-ha, the student learns four or five in each dastgah and goes
on to popular composed pieces, such as the tasnif and pish-
daramad.

The order in which the gusheh-ha are played is loosely defined
by tradition and is contained in the radif. There is even considerable agreement among the different versions of the radif regarding
this traditional order of gusheh-ha. The order usually follows a
curve, starting from the lowest part of the dastgah's range and
rising gradually until a high point is reached, with each gusheh
encompassing a slightly higher range. At the end of the performance, there is a descent to the starting tetrachord. For instance,
in the dastgah of Sehgah, it is customary to begin the performance
with the daramad, which is in the lowest tetrachord, and progress
to the gusheh-ha of Zabol, Muyeh, and Mokhalef, then return
to the first tetrachord. See Example 71 (the note shown as a
quarter note receives the most stress in each gusheh).

EXAMPLE 71.

Daramad   Zabol   Muyeh   Mokhalef   Sehgah

This procedure occurs in the *theory* of practice. The *practice*
of practice may well disregard the traditional order of gusheh-ha.
I discovered this to my chagrin when giving a lecture on Persian
music to an audience of non-Persians in Tehran. After
explaining the dastgah of Sehgah and the three most important
gusheh in great detail and illustrating each one, I asked my
teacher to perform. Beforehand we had agreed that he would
play the same dastgah as I had played and the same gusheh-ha

4. See chapter 4.

(the difference being, of course, that as a professional musician, not a student, his performance would be improvised). While he was playing, I found that I could not follow the sections of his performance. The audience, which was totally unfamiliar with this repertory, must have been at an even greater loss. Later, when I analyzed a tape recording of the performance with this player, he casually informed me that he had not begun in the first tetrachord of Sehgah and had not progressed to Zabol, Muyeh, and Mokhalef as is the traditional procedure. Rather, under the inspiration of the moment, he began in Mokhalef and, aside from short excursions back to the main tetrachord of Sehgah, had stayed in Mohkalef (which means "contrary") for his entire performance.

After this experience, I was prepared to hear the unexpected. However, in Iran not even inconsistency is consistent! When one of the most famous players in Iran was asked to tell what he had just played, he showed no hesitation in describing what I thought was a spontaneous performance. He produced an old piece of folded paper from his wallet and calmly read the names of the gusheh-ha of the dastgah he had just performed, and must have been performing in that order for a number of years.[5]

After deciding on the order of gusheh-ha, the performer must determine the number of pieces to play in each gusheh. For a solo performance of a dastgah of average length, that is, ten to fifteen minutes, many players open with a pish-daramad (before the daramad), a measured piece.[6] Following the pish-daramad is the daramad section, which may contain anywhere from one to six pieces called daramad, plus several other small sections. In the next gusheh, the performer may play only one piece, or, if it

5. In the traditional Persian musical setting where the musician is playing for a small group of friends, his performance is truly extemporaneous. But today, with the use of Persian art music in a more commercial environment, a musician frequently plans much of his improvisation beforehand in order to conform to the required time limits. The musician in the incident recounted above is a frequent performer on the radio.

Another way in which the theory of practice may differ from the practice of practice is that the range limitations characteristic of each gusheh may be disregarded. Octave transposition, coloratura passages, and figuration derived from Western-style music, such as arpeggios extending over several octaves, are techniques used by younger players that obscure the traditional range of each gusheh.

6. See chapter 5.

is an important gusheh, several, including a virtuoso piece called the chahar-mezrab (four beats).[7] A long performance will consist of many gusheh-ha with several sections in each; a shorter one, of only a few. There is normally a short pause between pieces. The ending of the dastgah performance may be extremely sudden, consisting of a short descent to the tonic tetrachord, or forud, or the player may prepare his descent elaborately and then play a measured piece, perhaps a reng (dance).[8]

For the shortest performance that is still representational—that is, one containing the most important gusheh-ha—at least five minutes would be required. A longer performance is, of course, much more satisfactory. Given more time, the player can establish the mood of the dastgah and warm up both his instrumental technique and his audience. Because the possibilities with each melody are vast and a master can invent countless variations within the framework of the dastgah, a great player can easily spend an hour on one section. Traditional performances in private homes may use one dastgah for the entire evening with several musicians performing their own versions.

Although it is customary to remain in a single dastgah for the entire performance, this too is not an inviolable rule. Master performers know a whole series of progressions that lead from one dastgah into another dastgah through related gusheh-ha. These are used both in the improvised music of the radif and in the composed forms. For example, the gusheh of Oshaq is found in the dastgah of Homayun, Esfahan, Dashti, Nava, and Rast Panjgah. Just as a common chord serves as a pivot between two different tonalities in Western music, this common gusheh can be a pivot taking the performer from one dastgah to a second dastgah and back to the first.[9]

Going to the other extreme, it is not uncommon to use a single gusheh for an entire performance. Some of the most important gusheh-ha have several sections and contain a large quantity of melodic material. A few of these larger gusheh-ha are slowly gaining the status of the auxiliary dastgah-ha, Esfahan, Dashti,

7. See pp. 131–135.
8. See pp. 146–147.
9. R. Khaleqi, "Modulation dar Musiqi-ye Irani," *Majaleh-ye Musiqi* 60–61 (1961).

Abu Ata, Bayat-e Tork, and Afshari. For example, the lengthy gusheh of Shushtari, from the dastgah of Homayun, is often played independently from Homayun and is likely to become a more important component of the dastgah system in the near future.

THE GUSHEH AS A BASIS FOR IMPROVISATION

The selection of gusheh-ha and their order is but a small part of the improvisation procedure. A more significant aspect of improvisation is the group of decisions determining how each gusheh is to be played. I have stressed that the gusheh is a kind of melodic model or a melodic framework, more or less elaborated depending upon the master from whom one learns it. The musician may alter and embellish the gusheh at will, and, theoretically, he performs it in a different way each time he plays. According to his feelings of the moment, the player creates a highly personal and intimate performance by varying and adding to the basic gusheh.

Thus, one may think of a gusheh as consisting of two sets of elements—one set of fixed elements and another set that varies for each performer and for each performance. These two sets of elements were identified over a thousand years ago by the philosopher and theorist al-Farabi: "Les éléments qui nous permettent de réaliser une mélodie sont de deux sortes: les uns constituent son existence essentielle; les autres rendent son existence plus parfaite. Il en est d'une mélodie comme de tout être né de l'association de plusieurs choses. Les éléments indispensables à sa réalisation sont les notes de l'espèce choisie et quant à ceux qui la rendent plus parfaite, les uns l'enrichissent d'autres y ajoutent des ornements ou de l'emphase."[10]

The fixed elements of the gusheh make up the model: the location and configuration of the tetrachord, the melodic function of each scale degree, the melodic shape, and characteristic cadence formulae. Illustrating these fixed elements is the melody for the initial gusheh of Shur, the daramad (see Example 72). Located in the lowest part of the Shur range, the daramad encompasses the tetrachord C D♭ E♭ F, which contains two neutral seconds, C

10. D'Erlanger, *MA*, II, 50.

to D-koron and D-koron to E-flat. The shahed and the ist are both the tonic note, C. The melody, in most versions, first stresses the C, then outlines the descent from the third and fourth notes to C, and again stresses this note. Its contour is primarily descending. This is the melodic model or the set of fixed elements for the daramad of Shur.[11] In an improvised performance, they would be recognizable.

The variable elements of the gusheh, those that are subject to each musician's individual choice, consist of elaborations and extensions on the basic melodic framework of the gusheh. In examining these it becomes useful to distinguish three primary categories of elaboration techniques: repetition and varied repetition, ornamentation, and centonization, or the joining together of familiar motives to produce longer melodies.

Repetition, a decorative feature extremely characteristic of Persian visual arts, can be noticed immediately in Persian carpets, in tile work on the domes of mosques, and in Persian miniature paintings. In its use of repetition, music resembles other Persian arts, as Persian musicians do not hesitate to repeat whole phrases without a single alteration. In fact, the printed literature is full of signs to indicate repetition.

A gusheh containing a large quantity of literal repetition is the fourth daramad of the dastgah Shur as given in the Maʿruffi radif (see Example 73). (Note that in this example, the dastgah of Shur is located on the note G rather than transposed to C as in the examples above. Throughout the rest of the present chapter, Shur will be presented as it is found in the Maʿruffi radif on G.)

EXAMPLE 72.   Maʿruffi, *MTI*, p. 2. (g′)

11. The fixed elements comprising the model are never isolated. We may say that the model of the gusheh is an abstraction existing only in theory books. Not even a student learns a gusheh in model form. What he memorizes, from his teacher's example or from a teaching manual, is an elaborated model, a partially finished composition, similar to those in the Saba or Maʿruffi radif-ha.

EXAMPLE 73.

EXAMPLE 74.   Saba, *DAS*, p. 26

EXAMPLE 75.   Saba, *DAS*, p. 11

An especially common type of repetition is the zir-bamm (high-low) technique, where the entire phrase is simply repeated one octave higher or lower. This change of register is quite refreshing after long sections of a performance that have been limited in compass to a single tetrachord (see Example 74). A refinement of repetition is the sequence—repetition of a phrase or motive on the next highest or lowest degree of the scale. Sequences are quite common in Persian music, especially for the sections of melismas called tahrir (trill, or ornamentation). See Example 75.

Varied repetition, the broadest category of this technique, includes rhythmic and melodic modification of the basic motive. It is well illustrated in the growth of the three-note motive that is the basic unit in the Shur daramad. According to the version of Maʿruffi, the motive in its first and simplest appearance is given in Example 76. As a nuclear pattern of three notes, it appears with rhythmic modifications in Examples 77 and 78.

EXAMPLE 76.

EXAMPLE 77.

EXAMPLE 78.

Melodic modification includes addition of accessory notes and of ornaments. In the process of enlarging the basic motive, there are changes of emphasis and articulation, including the device of withholding the note of stress, here the G, and thus increasing the tension of the phrase. See Examples 79–85. The last three examples feature the tahrir, the characteristic Middle East melisma.

EXAMPLE 79.

EXAMPLE 80.

EXAMPLE 81.

EXAMPLE 82.

EXAMPLE 83.

EXAMPLE 84.

EXAMPLE 85.

Ornamentation, like repetition, is an element characteristic of all Persian art. This is well known in the visual arts where "everything, whether made for common or ceremonial use, is lavishly enlivened with ornament ... Such enrichment is no mere space-serving artifice for masking bare forms, but an essential part of fine craftsmanship, without which a work is incomplete."[12] In Persian music no less than in the visual arts, ornamentation is a vital necessity.[13] Indeed, one may almost say

12. A. H. Christie, "Islamic Minor Arts," *The Legacy of Islam*, ed. Thomas Arnold and Alfred Guillaume (Oxford, 1952), p. 112.

13. "Here [in the East] the ornament is not additional, but a component force setting into motion the dead degrees of scales toward the formation of primary patterns of melody. [It is] needless to recall the strong inclination of Eastern musicians to start an ornamental rotation around the structural notes in a given modality. There appears to be endless movement within the quiescence of a linear art without shadows, perspectives, and synamism; again, one cannot but compare it with the huge surfaces of ancient carpets covered with hundreds of small compartments all of them filled with ornamental

that not a single note is left unornamented, for every note longer than an eighth note is strummed, and if a note is not strummed, it is trilled. Strums and trills are so common that they are not indicated by special signs in the notation but are understood by the player. Example 86 shows how single notes in Western notation would be interpreted by a santur player.

EXAMPLE 86.   Saba, *DAS*, pp. 5–6

Among the ornaments indicated by special signs in the notation, grace notes are extremely common. A small circle indicates that the note is to be preceded by a grace note one step higher than the previous note. A figure 3 following the sign indicates that the grace note is a third higher; 4, a fourth, and so forth. Whole strings of grace notes, especially in descending passages, are favored by Persian performers (see Example 87). Other signed ornaments are illustrated in Example 88.[14]

Centonization, or the joining together of recognizable motives, is a technique most likely to occur at cadences, as in the fourth daramad of the Maʿruffi Shur (see Example 89). In the rhythm of the first four notes, repeated twice, is quoted a melody

---

motives which are of a uniform style yet never repeated. Obviously, the creative impetus is similar in both arts, and it is up to us to learn how to follow their paths." Edith Gerson-Kiwi, *The Persian Doctrine of Dastga-Composition* (Tel-Aviv, 1963), pp. 22–23.

14. Some ornaments important in Western music are not found in Persian music. For example, because the melodic movement in Persian music is so diatonic, nonstructural passing notes are not used. Also, those ornaments whose function depends on strict metric regularity—divisions of a basic time unit, suspensions, appoggiaturas—are absent.

Ornamentation in Persian architecture.

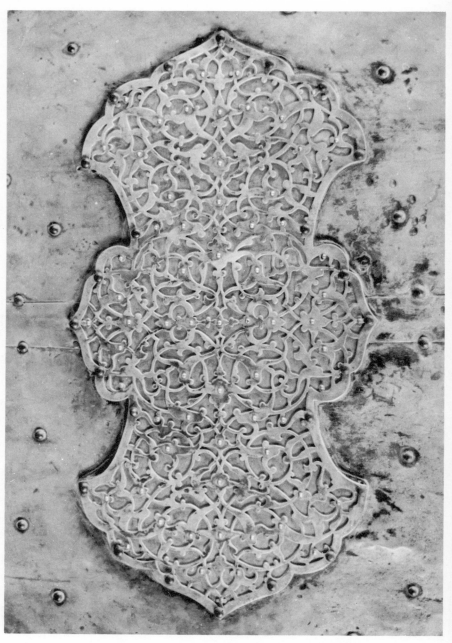

Ornamentation in Persian metal work and ceramic tile.

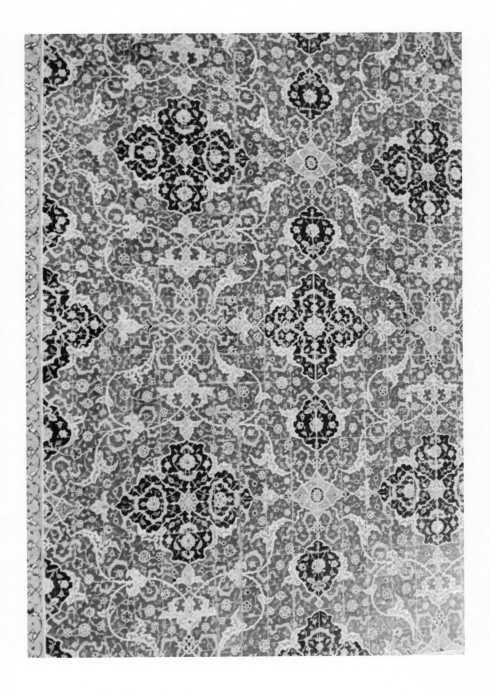

frequently played in Shur.[15] To extend the piece beyond this short melody, Maʿruffi joins a group of motives that have been used frequently in the preceding short pieces of the daramad section (from the dotted vertical line).

EXAMPLE 87.   Saba, *DDS*, p. 5

EXAMPLE 88.   Saba, *DAS*, pp. 4–7

15. It is also found in the Saba and Borumand radif. See Example 4 above.

EXAMPLE 89.

TECHNIQUES OF ELABORATION

The process of creating a composition through improvisation works on two levels: first, the elaboration of the nuclear theme using the techniques described above to create a short piece; then, a combining of a number of pieces to make up the subsection of the dastgah called the gusheh. We may observe this process by analyzing the first gusheh of Shur in the Maʿruffi radif.[16] Among the fourteen small pieces in this extensive gusheh, five are called daramad, with the remainder bearing more specific names, such as kereshmeh, chahar mezrab, and hazine.

The first daramad, Example 90, has been discussed above where its range of a tetrachord made of two neutral seconds was emphasized. In the transposition of Shur on G, which is being used throughout this discussion, the tetrachord is G, A-koron, B-flat, and C. Both the note of stress and that of cadence are G. The melodic shape of the daramad was described as trisectional: the first part stresses the tonic; the second emphasizes the descents from B-flat and from C to the tonic; the third, similar to the first, stresses the tonic with stereotyped cadence patterns. These three sections are functionally distinguished. The first and third are static, the medial is more dynamic.[17]

16. This source has been chosen to illustrate the process of improvisation not only because it is accessible in the volume *MTI*, but also because this author judges it to be extremely close to live performances. Confirmation of this may be found by comparing these examples with transcriptions of live performances in Hormoz Farhat, "The Dastgah Concept in Persian Music" (PhD. diss., University of California, Los Angeles, 1965).

17. In Schenkerian terms, the medial section is more dominant in function; in fact, it often ends with a semicadence on the second degree.

EXAMPLE 90.

EXAMPLE 91.

EXAMPLE 92.

EXAMPLE 93.

EXAMPLE 94.

This basic melody of Shur is elaborated in the four daramad-ha in Examples 91–94 by the techniques of repetition, ornamentation, and centonization described above. As succeeding daramad-ha become more elaborated, their length increases.[18] Thus, the first daramad lasts approximately sixteen seconds, while the fifth is ninety-four seconds. The increase is found in each of the units of musical development, the motive, the phrase, and the section. The growth of the basic three-note motive of Shur was observed in Examples 76–85 above; other important motives show a corresponding growth. The next larger unit, the phrase, is lengthened by repetition of these longer motives and by a delaying of the tonic through sequences and melismas. Finally, sections are lengthened by repeating the longer phrases. In the later daramad-ha, sections of four phrases often form an AABA pattern.

Accompanying this increase in length among the five daramad is a corresponding increase in range, later daramad-ha showing a gradual widening of the range to stress the upper notes of the tetrachord. For example, whereas the first and second daramad mentioned the fourth note, C, only as auxiliary to the note B, by the fifth daramad, C is stressed quite heavily, with its upper neighbor, D, mentioned several times.

Thus, the daramad-ha differ among each other in length, range, and amount of embellishment. There is usually a distinct difference in rhythm also, with one rhythmic figure predominant in one

18. The fourth daramad, a familiar melody, is an exception to this lengthening.

daramad and another in a second. For example, in the Saba radif for santur, each daramad features a different rhythm.

The five daramad of Maʿruffi are, in effect, five new pieces. But even though the daramad-ha are indeed different pieces, they may also be regarded as merely five different ways of expressing the same musical idea. All five share the same four-note range, the same melodic contour, the same diatonic motion, the same tonic, the same lack of metric regularity, and even some of the same motives. In addition, the three general sections of the daramad are preserved, and in the longer daramad-ha become similar to an exposition, development, and recapitulation. Among the five daramad, one of the most important similarities is the principle of stressed tones. In all five, the note G is most important, with the note B-flat second.[19] The function of each note in the tetrachord is extremely important to the performer. Barkechli states that the notes of stress serve as guideposts to orient the performer throughout his improvisation, while Dariouche Safvate calls the gusheh a "little demonstration around the important notes of the scale."[20]

In summary, the creation of small pieces in the daramad section can be regarded as the performer's individual way of extending the basic material of the gusheh. To create a composition, each player uses his stock of filler material—rhythmic units, embellishments, and so forth. Even if the filler material is part of the traditional stock, its use is particular to the performer. There seems to be a greater difference between the same numbered daramad belonging to different performers than between different daramad-ha of the same player. Since these melody types are still part of an oral tradition, different performers may have a different conception of the model or stress one particular aspect of the gusheh more than another.

If the creating of daramad-ha through elaboration of the basic melodic model is considered to be the first level in improvisation, on a somewhat different level is the next step, the gathering

19. The importance of the third in dastgah-e Shur is emphasized by Khatchi Khatchi in "Das Intervallbildungsprinzip des persischen Dastgah Shur," *Jahrbuch für musikalische Volks- und Völkerkünde* 3 (1967), pp. 70-84.

20. Mehdi Barkechli, *MTI*, p. 38; Dariouche Safvate, in conversation in 1963.

together of small pieces to form the gusheh or a movement of the dastgah composition. In addition to the daramad-ha, which develop the basic idea of the gusheh in free rhapsodic style, there are pieces that have individual names and a special style and that usually have had strict metric regularity. Hormoz Farhat has greatly aided the analysis of these pieces by giving them the generic name tekke-ha (pieces).[21] Tekke-ha may be played in any of the twelve dastgah, for while they have either a distinct melodic or rhythmic identity, they have no modal identity; they adopt the mode of the dastgah or gusheh in which they are played.

In the Maᶜruffi radif, of the fourteen pieces in the opening gusheh of Shur, five are daramad-ha and nine are tekke-ha. The configuration is as follows:

1. Moqadameh (introduction)　　A generic name for introduc-
　　　　　　　　　　　　　　　　　tion. The piece is unmeas-
　　　　　　　　　　　　　　　　　ured, slow, and rather
　　　　　　　　　　　　　　　　　stately in character.

2. Daramad-e aval (first
　　daramad)
3. Daramad-e dovom (second
　　daramad)
4. Daramad-e sevom (third
　　daramad)
5. Daramad-e chaharom
　　(fourth daramad)
6. Kereshmeh (nod or wink)　　An important measured piece
　　　　　　　　　　　　　　　　　found in many dastgah-ha.
　　　　　　　　　　　　　　　　　There is always a strong
　　　　　　　　　　　　　　　　　hemiola effect throughout.

7. Gusheh-ye Rohab
8. Kereshmeh
9. Daramad-e panjom (fifth
　　daramad)
10. Kereshmeh

21. Farhat, Dastgah Concept, p. 243.

11. Avaz (song)	A general term used to indicate an unmeasured piece. Here the avaz is a well known melody.
12. Chahar mezrab (four beats)	A virtuoso piece, rapid and measured.[22]
13. Naghmeh (melody)	A term used by Maʿruffi for a piece that involves much repetition and oscillation between two notes.
14. Hazine (sad)	Another piece with a repeated-note motive. It has a range of a minor sixth and often cadences on the fourth above.

Although each of these tekke-ha has its own prominent stylistic features, all are part of one gusheh in this composition by Maʿruffi, the opening gusheh of Shur, or the daramad. Thus, they share with the five pieces actually named *daramad* and with each other the same melodic contour and the same modal characteristics—an identical range, scale, intervals and notes of stress and stopping.[23] Example 95, the tekke kereshmeh, the sixth piece in this gusheh, illustrates the resemblance of the tekke to the daramad of Shur.

How a tekke is dependent on the gusheh where it is played may be further stressed by comparing this kereshmeh in Shur with a kereshmeh from another dastgah. Example 96 is a kereshmeh from Chahargah, transcribed to center on the same note as the kereshmeh from Shur. Both pieces have the hemiola rhythm characteristic of the tekke kereshmeh. But the melodic contours and modal characteristics reflect those of the daramad-ha of Shur and Chahargah respectively: Shur's kereshmeh starts on the seventh scale degree and stresses the tonic, while that of Chahargah starts on the fourth below the tonic and skips a third to the tonic.

22. See chapter 5.
23. Other important tekke-ha that are not found in this example are the reng (pp. 146–147, the Masnavi, and the zarbi. In addition, Farhat describes five other tekke: bastenegar, zangule, dobeyti, and jamedaran. "The Dastgah Concept," pp. 243–252.

Further comparison can be made between these tekke-ha and the examples of the daramad-ha in chapter 3.[24]

In the Ma‘ruffi radif, the first gusheh or the first movement of dastgah Shur was an extremely long movement consisting of fourteen pieces. A more common kind of structure, used as a gusheh in the Saba radif, which is not nearly as elaborate as that of Ma‘ruffi, is a single piece presented in three sections:[25] Introduction; melody (sheir, meaning "poetry"; the verses of the poem are printed in the Saba radif even though it is for instrumental performance); and coda (tahrir). These three parts are usually found in a single piece (see Example 97), although they may be extended into two or three short pieces.

EXAMPLE 95.   Ma‘ruffi, *MTI*, p. 6

24. Shur and Chahargah, chapter 3.
25. This structure was brought to my attention by Faramarz Payvar.

EXAMPLE 96. Maʿruffi, *MTI*, p. 5. (c′)

EXAMPLE 97.   "Shushtari." Saba, *DDS*, pp. 11–12

The preceding analysis of improvisation concerns solo instrumental performance. What happens when the instrumentalist
joins a vocalist, or a vocalist and drummer, for the ensemble
typical of Persian art music? What controls exist to keep the
performance organized?

In the ensemble, all players relinquish a measure of their
independence to the singer who is the acknowledged leader of
the group. Decisions of the improvisation process relating to the
choice of dastgah and gusheh-ha are usually planned beforehand,
as are the number of small pieces to be performed in each gusheh.
But choices about the performance of each small piece within the
gusheh are left to the singer. For the major part of the performance, the player follows the singer rather closely, echoing the
phrase last sung with perhaps a slight variation. The resulting
texture is heterophonic. The instrumentalist has passages of free
improvisation between verses of the poetry, and there is usually at
least one break for solo drum improvisation.

The structure of an improvised composition with voice and
instrument may be illustrated by analyzing the performance of
dastgah Shur on Folkways recording FW 8831.[26] The six verses
of poetry, preceded by an introduction, are set to the following
gusheh-ha: daramad 1, daramad 2, Salmak, Shahnaz, Razavi, and
daramad 2.[27] The entire piece contains fifteen sections divided as
follows:

Section	Title	Performer
1. Gusheh 1	Daramad 1	Santur
2. Gusheh 1	Daramad 1	Voice
3. Gusheh 1	Daramad 1	Santur
4. Gusheh 2	Daramad 2	Voice
5. Gusheh 2	Daramad 2	Santur
6. Gusheh 3	Salmak	Voice
7. Gusheh 3	Salmak	Santur
8. Gusheh 4	Shahnaz	Voice (tahrir)
9. Gusheh 4	Shahnaz	Santur

26. "Classical Music of Iran." The performers are Khatereh Parvaneh, singer, and
Mohammad Heydari, santur player.
27. The names *Salmak* and *Razavi* were given by the performer.

10. Gusheh 4	Shahnaz	Voice
11. Gusheh 4	Shahnaz	Santur
12. Gusheh 4	Shahnaz	Voice (tahrir closes this section)
13. Gusheh 4	Shahnaz	Santur
14. Gusheh 5	Razavi	Voice (tahrir closes this section and begins the forud to Shur)
15. Gusheh 6	Daramad 2	Voice

In this chapter I have attempted to rationalize the process of improvisation in the use of the radif. If the radif is considered to be "information" acquired by the performer through his training, the performance is then the player's *use* of this information for his improvisation. In accordance with a layer of theory that might be labeled "theory of practice," there are certain procedures for using this information. Tradition generally dictates the choice and order of gusheh-ha in a dastgah, the method of proceeding from gusheh to gusheh, and the methods of extending and ornamenting the melodic line.

After considering all these procedures, however, one must admit that the performer is not bound by them. For, in Persian music, the essential factors in a performance are the feelings of the player and those of his audience. At the actual time of performance, the musician does not calculate the procedures that will guide his playing. Rather he plays from a level of consciousness somewhat removed from the purely rational. Sometimes he may achieve a trancelike state through his playing (or through other artificial means). Under these conditions the player performs not according to the "theory of practice," but intuitively, according to the "practice of practice," wherein the dictates of traditional procedures are integrated with his immediate mood and emotional needs.

5 The Practice of Persian Art Music: Rhythm and Form

In comparing the traditional art music of Persia with that of her neighbors to the east and to the west, it is at once apparent that Persian music is far less measured rhythmically than either Indian or Arabian music. In these musics most of a performance is measured, and a well defined rhythmic pattern is strongly felt. Only the introductory sections—alapa in Indian music and taqsim in Arabian music—have rubato playing. Persian music, on the other hand, is not measured throughout but contains long sections of unmeasured, free rubato playing similar to the alapa and taqsim. This great rhythmic freedom, conducive to improvisation, allows for the abundant ornamentation characteristic of Persian art.

Although much of Persian music is unmeasured, a traditional performance contains both unmeasured and measured pieces with the unmeasured type, as a class called avaz (song), predominating.[1] In the radif of Mussa Maᶜruffi, for example, out of a total of 470 pieces, only 109 are measured, while in the several versions of the radif of Abol Hassan Saba, approximately one third are measured. Recent practice, however, has increased the quantity of measured playing, especially among younger musicians. Both types of pieces will be examined here, beginning with the more traditional unmeasured class, avaz. As the avaz is

---

1. The term avaz is also used instead of naghmeh to indicate an auxiliary dastgah. As much of the terminology in music is inconsistent, different theorists often use different words for the same concept.

primarily a vocal form, the use of poetry in Persian music will also be considered in this section.

Unmeasured Pieces

When a musician plays the unmeasured pieces of the radif, he has extensive freedom, for a fluid unmeasured line allows almost unlimited rhythmic leniency, or rubato, the tempo and the lengths of the pauses being completely subject to his immediate feelings. If the performer is particularly inspired, the avaz is likely to be played more slowly, to be drawn out, with long, emotion-filled pauses. A routine performance is more perfunctory, and long notes will be trilled only briefly with less pause between phrases. For example, the opening of the dastgah Sehgah (Example 75) could be played in about fifteen seconds, or it could take as long as forty-five.[2]

To analyze the element of rhythm in unmeasured Persian pieces one must turn to poetry; for traditional Persian music, like the music of ancient Greece is based on words. A performance without singing is more the exception than the rule. Persians generally consider music incomplete if there is no poetry.[3] The radif is customarily set to verses of classical poetry written by the thirteenth-century poets Saꞔadi and Rumi and the fourteenth-century poet Hafez. As was mentioned in the discussion of the theory of rhythm in chapter 2, meter in Persian poetry is extremely well defined. With training in the science of ꞔaruz,[4] a musician may scan poetry using the system of faꞔayl, learning to recognize the various meters. For connoisseurs of vocal music, the best singers are those who can analyze the meter of the poetry and then set it to music in a way that preserves that meter and does not conflict with it. But according to contem-

---

2. Two rhythmic factors are less subject to the performer's individual interpretation, or are weakly defined by tradition: the rhythmic articulation of the phrase and the rhythmic execution of the ornaments. At present, the usual notation of Persian music does not represent these factors adequately, and the student learns them by rote from his master.

3. In the Saba instruction manuals, the poetry is written out for each avaz even though these pieces are for solo instrument. Furthermore, many instrument teachers insist that the students learn to sing these pieces as well as play them.

4. See also GenꞋichi Tsuge, "Rhythmic Aspects of the *Avaz* in Persian Music," *Ethnomusicology* 14 (May 1970), 205–227.

porary observers, such singers are now rare in Iran. One writer has likened today's singers to actors who recite their lines correctly but use completely wrong facial expressions; that is, singers today ignore the meter of the poetry and set it to music incorrectly.[5]

Thus it is the meter of the poetry that most often gives a rhythmic shape to the unmeasured avaz, the sections of the piece with poetry being more rhythmically articulated than the free sections of trills or instrumental passages. It is even possible to notate the parts of the piece that contain poetry with measure lines. Examples 98, 99, and 100 show possible musical settings for one verse from three poems.

Example 98, a couplet by the poet Hafez, is in the mujtas meter: ◡‒◡‒ ◡◡‒‒ ◡‒◡‒ ◡◡‒‒. Here the last foot is shortened to ‒ ‒ instead of ◡◡ ‒ ‒. The onomatopoetic scansion is: mafāᶜilun faᶜilātun mafāᶜilun fālun. The musical setting is a measured one, in the popular rhythm known as kereshmeh. It is completely syllabic except for notes joined with a slur.

Bĭ-yā vă kesh-tĭ-ye mā dar shă-tē-ye shăr-āb ăn-dāz

Khŏr-ūsh vă ve-lŭ-lĕh dar jăn-ĕ sheikh vă shăb ăn-dāz.

Come and let us cast our boat into the river of wine
Let us cast a shout and clamor into the soul of the sheikh and the young man.

EXAMPLE 98.   Saba, *DSS*, p. 7

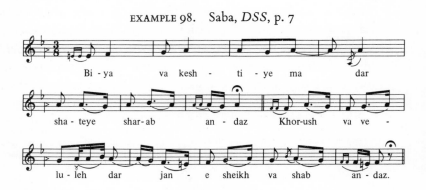

5. A remark made in conversation by Mehdi Forugh, professor of drama at Tehran University who has written a long series of articles on the relation of poetry to music. See note 16 below.

The most important poet for classical music is undoubtedly
Jalal ed din Rumi, for settings of his *Masnavi* are found as tekke-ha
in more than half of the twelve dastgah systems.[6] These poems are
always in ramal meter, ＿∪＿＿ ＿∪＿＿ ＿∪＿＿, although the
musical setting does not preserve the meter strictly. An unusually
clear example is part of the *Masnavi* from Bayat-e Tork in the
radif of Saba (see Example 99). Notes joined by a slur in the score
are used for only one syllable of text.

Chun-ke gol raft va go-les-tan shod khar-ab [♪]

Bu-ye gol-ra az ke ju-yim az gol-ab. [♪]

Because the flower is gone the garden is destroyed
If we wish to seek the smell of the flower it is in rose-water.

EXAMPLE 99.   Saba, *DDS*, p. 8

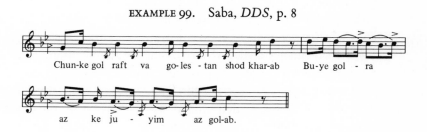

Example 100, a more typical example, illustrates the freedom
of musical setting and also the process of elaboration. Here in
Masnavi Mokhalef, the musical setting follows the meter of the
poetry but is more elaborate rhythmically than the Masnavi
setting in Example 99. Note the tahrir (trill) at the end of each
phrase.

'Ash-e-qy pey-dast-(o) az za-ri- ye del [ꟻ]

Nist -(o) bi-ma-ri chu bi-ma—r-ye del [ꟻ]

The grieving of the heart announces the state of love
And there is no illness like that of the heart.

6. The *Masnavi* have been translated by A. J. Arberry, *Tales from the Masnavi* (London,
1961) and *More Tales from the Masnavi* (London, 1963). See also the section on poetry
below.

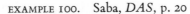

EXAMPLE 100. Saba, *DAS*, p. 20

'Ash-e-qy   pey-dast-(o) az   za-ri-ye del

Nist-(o) bi-ma-ri   chu bi-ma-ri-ye

del.

Although on first hearing, the rhythmic organization of a dastgah composition may not be noticeable, analysis of the performance will often reveal its rhythmic structure. For the dependence of the music on poetry has an even broader rhythmic significance, going beyond the individual piece. Usually, in a vocal performance of a dastgah, one poem is used and all the lines of that poem have approximately the same meter.[7] In the vocal performance analyzed above, lines of the poem are sung at regular intervals, with improvised instrumental sections and long vocal melismas between the lines. As noted, the rhythm of each line of music is determined by the meter of the poem. Because this meter is constant throughout the poem, the vocal sections thus have a rhythmic similarity and create a rhythmic unity in the performance. Even when there is no singer, the solo instrumentalist may play these sections of avaz as if the poetry were being sung. Thus, the poem gives rise to a recurrent rhythmic structure in what appears to be, to the uninitiated listener, a completely unmeasured performance. In the following list, the predominant rhythm is labeled *Rhythm 2*.

The Rhythmic Structure of a Typical Performance

Introduction	Unmeasured rhythm
or	or
Chahar mezrab	Rhythm 1

7. There is evidence of an old tradition of specific classical poems appropriate to specific dastgah-ha or gusheh-ha. Although this tradition is no longer followed, it may explain some of the rhythmic figures characteristic of each dastgah. A number of poems and their suggested setting, i.e., the names of the melodies, are given by Mirza Nasir Forsat-e Dowleh in *Bohur el Alhan* (Tehran, 1953).

Gusheh 1	Poetry	Rhythm 2
	Tahrir (trill)	Unmeasured
Gusheh 2	Poetry	Rhythm 2
	Instrumental interlude	Unmeasured
Gusheh 3	Poetry	Rhythm 2
	Longer instrumental interlude	Rhythm 3
Gusheh 4	Poetry	Rhythm 2
	Tahrir	Unmeasured
	Instrumental conclusion	Rhythm 4

Although the unmeasured avaz is the most traditional way of performing the radif, it is said to be difficult to perform well. Hence many performers today do not learn avaz, but concentrate on rhythmic pieces such as tasnif and pish-daramad.

Measured Pieces[8]

Of all the measured pieces in a performance of classical Persian music, by far the most important is the chahar mezrab (four beats). Every dastgah composition contains several chahar mezrab-ha, located not only in the opening tetrachord but also in the tetrachords of the important gusheh-ha. Since it is the most brilliant and exciting part of the composition, the chahar mezrab provides an excellent opportunity for the player to demonstrate his virtuosity.

Like fugue, the chahar mezrab is a style of playing, not a form. Characteristic of this style is a rapid tempo and an ostinato figure, the payeh (foundation, or base), which is established at the opening of the piece and continued throughout. Almost always, the payeh contains a pedal tone,[9] and over the payeh, a melody is sounded (see Example 101).

8. Some of the specific rhythms used in these measured pieces are mentioned by Nelly Caron and Dariouche Safvate, *Iran: Les traditions musicales* (Buchet/Chastel, 1966), pp. 133–140.

9. Continual reference to a single tonic, reminiscent of the drone in Indian music, is even more common in the provincial music of eastern Iran. Players of the ghaychek in Baluchistan sound the melody on the top string of their instrument and use the next lower strings to sound a drone of a fifth. In the same region of the country there are wind instruments with two separate sections, one for the melody and the other for the drone.

EXAMPLE 101.   The opening of a chahar mezrab from Dashti. Saba, *DDS*, p. 23

The kind of ostinato pattern and the manner of repeating the pedal tone are different for each instrument. Just as a virtuoso piece for violin would not be the same as one for piano, each Persian instrument has its own characteristic style of chahar mezrab with its own particular figurations. The chahar mezrab played on the santur, shown in Example 101, features wide spacing and repeated notes; one played on the violin often has double stops and a rapid bowing figuration called archet (bow). See Example 102.

EXAMPLE 102.   The opening of a chahar mezrab from Bayat-e Tork. Saba, *DDV*, p. 20

The name of this type of composition raises a problem. Translated literally, chahar mezrab means "four beats." But, without exception, chahar mezrab-ha are in triple meter, 6/16 or 3/8. Khatchi Khatchi explains the origin of the name as derived from the technical terminology of the tar. Since the strings of the tar are tuned in pairs, each note on the instrument is simultaneously sounded on two strings. In the chahar mezrab there are two notes at each instant, the pedal note and the melody note. Thus, Khatchi claims, the name *four beats* comes from the nearly simultaneous striking of four strings when the chahar mezrab is played on the tar.[10] But one difficulty with this suggestion is that the word *mezrab* does not mean "string." A more likely solution is simply that a duple meter is felt strongly, at least at the beginning of the piece. Furthermore, the melodic unit is usually two measures, causing four beats to predominate (see Example 102). Later in the composition, this rhythm may be purposely distorted to form syncopations.

The melodic material of the chahar mezrab is taken directly from the radif. If one compares a chahar mezrab and an unmeasured gusheh from a single dastgah, the same general melodic outline can be observed in both. In Example 103, a chahar mezrab from Shur, the melody created by the notes in the lower register is similar, in essence, to that of the daramad in Example 72.

In summary, the style characteristics of the chahar mezrab are a rapid tempo, an ostinato pattern, a bourdon or pedal tone, and a

---

10. *Der Dastgah* (Regensburg, 1962), p. 151, n. 29.

EXAMPLE 103. The opening of a chahar mezrab in Shur. Saba, *DAS*, p. 22.

wide melodic compass. A chahar mezrab contains fairly simple melodic material, most often taken from the radif and characteristic of the dastgah in which the chahar mezrab is played. The importance of this form to contemporary Persian art music is twofold. First, it is strictly nonvocal. Since traditional Persian art music has been predominantly vocal, the recent development of instrumental styles takes on added significance. Secondly, the chahar mezrab is a genre between improvised and composed music. Many chahar mezrab-ha are still improvised,[11] but musicians

11. As noted by Hormoz Farhat, the kind of improvisation in the chahar mezrab "is in the order of repeating phrases or building melodic sequences on the existing phrases." "The Dastgah Concept in Persian Music" (PhD. diss., University of California, Los Angeles, 1965), p. 268.

also play those of other artists that have been published or recorded.

Apart from the chahar mezrab, which is the most important measured piece in the radif, there are other measured pieces employing rhythmic patterns. An example mentioned above is the piece called kereshmeh (nod, or wink) whose rhythm is found in nearly all the dastgah-ha, sometimes under different names. When poetry is set to music having this particular rhythm, the rhythm of the music is so strong that the rhythm of the poem takes second place, and the meter of the poetry may be slightly distorted. The majority of measured pieces in the radif that are not chahar mezrab-ha are in the kereshmeh rhythm (see Example 104).

EXAMPLE 104.   Kereshmeh in Shur. Maʿruffi, *MTI*, p. 3

Other measured pieces, which have a wide variety of different rhythms, are called, as a class, zarbi (rhythmic or measured). Example 105 is Zarbi Shushtari from Homayun.

EXAMPLE 105.   The opening of Zarbi Shushtari. Saba, *DSS*, p. 12

Surveying the radif of Persian music from the standpoint of rhythm, the predominance of unmeasured pieces was significant. But even in the unmeasured sections of the radif, a partial rhythmic structure often results from the use of strongly metered Persian poetry. In addition to the measured pieces that exist within the radif (chahar mezrab, kereshmeh, and zarbi), measured pieces are also found in the body of music outside the radif. These composed, nonimprovised pieces, which may be considered to occupy a place between "light classical" and "popular" music, are always measured and are strongly rhythmic.[12]

The unmeasured style of playing, which comprises most of the radif, is particularly well suited to a highly emotional, intensely personal and extemporaneous music. A player can transfer his feelings more directly and immediately into music when he does not have the limitations of a strictly measured, written form. Furthermore, this unmeasured style, inducing a feeling of vagueness and mysticism, is considered to be a perfect expression of the Persian soul.

But contemporary Iranian classical music, no longer strictly reserved for the traditional, intimate gatherings once typical of Iran, is now also played on radio and television. With this dramatic change of setting have come alterations in the character of the music. Indeed, within the last twenty-five years, the style of Iranian life has changed so radically that a mystic, unmeasured music now seems unsuitable.[13] It is usually the case that when a modern, movie-going, young Iranian reaches the age at which he would appreciate avaz, he has heard too much rhythmic music to like avaz. Thus, the amount of unmeasured avaz seems to be

---

12. See pp. 139–147.

13. Ruhollah Khaleqi once remarked to me that most avaz on the Tehran radio stations were scheduled for evening programs, when the frenzy of the city had calmed down.

decreasing with a corresponding increase in the measured styles.[14]

FORM

Today classical Persian music encompasses several different kinds of composition that might be called large musical forms. For this investigation they are divided into three categories: (1) improvised compositions, namely, the music of the radif; (2) composed pieces, namely, tasnif, pish-daramad, and reng; and (3) suites containing both improvised and composed pieces. The latter two categories have not been discussed previously, since they are one degree removed from traditional Persian art music. Of more recent origin than the radif, they tend to be of a less classical, hence more popular, character. The first category, the radif, familiar to the reader, is briefly reviewed here in its formal aspect, that is, in the sectionalization of the performance.

The Radif

When performing a dastgah, it is customary to start in the tonic tetrachord and play the most important gusheh-ha, that is, visit the most important "corners." The linking of gusheh to gusheh creates a formal structure delineated by several elements of music: a structure based on the progression of tetrachords, pitch levels, or tessituras; a vague thematic form based on a succession of melodic shapes; and a sectional grouping of the gusheh-ha as individual pieces, set off by a pause. In addition, each player creates another element of structure, one not predetermined by the radif but by the performer. This is based on an alternation of measured and unmeasured lengths of music, as when rhythmic chahar mezrab-ha played in two or three tetrachord areas create contrasting sections with the gusheh-ha in the unmeasured avaz style.

14. The current vogue of drum playing is a strong factor increasing the use of rhythm in Persian art music. In Eastern as well as Western music, the presence of a great instrumentalist in any given period creates an increase in the number of students for that instrument and also an increase in its literature. In Tehran today, a virtuoso drummer who ranks among the best musicians in the country is Hossein Tehrani, who has created a vogue for solo drum playing much in the style of Western jazz drummers. See pp. 174–175. The increase in measured styles is also correlated with an increase in nonimprovised pieces. See p. 194.

Additional formal possibilities result when the instrumentalist shares the performance with a singer and drummer, the most typical ensemble for performances of art music today. This ensemble follows the same pattern of starting in the tonic tetrachord and moving to the various gusheh-ha. But the strongest formal elements in vocal performances are the establishing of definite phrase lengths determined by the poetry and the alternations of vocal sections with instrumental ritornelli.

The alternation of vocal sections and instrumental ritornelli, illustrated by the analysis of a recorded performance of Shur in chapter 4, often results in the following kind of structure: The opening section belongs to the instrumentalist, who plays either a few measures or an extended introduction. The singer then performs the first section of poetry that belongs to the daramad. Here the accompaniment is heterophonic; the instrumentalist follows the singer and either echoes each phrase literally or plays a slight variation. The second daramad, if there is one, follows immediately. Between the daramad and the following gusheh there is usually a long vocal melisma, and a solo instrumental section. In a short performance, this procedure is repeated through three or four gusheh. Toward the end, the vocal melismas increase in length and virtuosity. In a long performance, perhaps eight or ten gusheh will be played, and the instrumentalist will perform a long solo about two-thirds of the way through, often accompanied by the drummer.

The fundamental unit in every species of classical Persian poetry is the beyt (couplet). Each of the two symmetrical lines of the beyt consist of six or eight feet, ending with the same rhyme.[15] And each couplet is of convenient length to be set by one gusheh. For instance, if the poem chosen for a performance had six couplets, and the dastgah chosen was Chahargah, the setting might be this:[16]

First couplet   First daramad of Chahargah
Second couplet   Second daramad of Chahargah

---

15. Edward G. Browne, *A Literary History of Persia* (Cambridge, 1928), II, 24.

16. Additional references for the problem of setting words to music may be found in the long series of articles by Mehdi Forugh in the Persian music journal *Majaleh-ye Musiqi*, nos. 17–32.

Third couplet	First daramad of the gusheh Zabol
Fourth couplet	Second daramad of Zabol
Fifth couplet	Daramad of Mokhalef
Sixth couplet	Forud (descent) to the tonic tetrachord of Chahargah

Composed Persian Music

The Tasnif. Of all the music played in the cities of Iran today, by far the most popular form is the tasnif (ballad). This is a broad form ranging from a Western art song, or lied, to a popular commercial song. What distinguishes the tasnif from other Persian vocal music, the singing found in the radif (avaz), is that while the avaz is unmeasured and improvisatory, the tasnif has a definite meter. It is also composed, although not necessarily notated. Furthermore, the poetry used for each type of singing is different. For the avaz, classical poetry is generally used. The tasnif, on the other hand, occasionally quotes single lines from classical sources but depends heavily on contemporary poetry or poetry composed within the last century. For this reason E. G. Browne defined the tasnif as a "topical ballad."[17] He traces its origin back to pre-Islamic Persia when in the courts of the Sassanian kings, famous minstrels such as Barbad sang of the events of the day. Another tasnif singer whose skill as a harpist is legendary is Rudaki, who lived early in the tenth century. Verses of Rudaki have survived, the most famous being those of the song he performed before the Samanid Prince to induce him to return to his native city of Bokhara.[18]

In the first decade of the twentieth century, a great number of topical satirical ballads were written, the majority of them in disguise—that is, with seemingly innocuous verses which acquired political or even revolutionary overtones only when sung. The greatest tasnif writers of this period were Aref and Sheyda.[19]

17. Browne, *Literary History of Persia*, I, 17.
18. Ibid., II, 15.
19. Because of his revolutionary sentiments, the tasnif writer Aref is especially cultivated by the Soviet Cultural Organization in Tehran. In 1964 his birthday was observed with a special program. A section of Khaleqi's history of Persian music is devoted to the tasnif (*SMI*, pp. 411–427); and for a more detailed discussion of the poetry used in tasnif-ha, see Hossein Alin Mallah, "Tasnif chist?" *Majaleh-ye Musiqi* 13–14 (1957).

Considering its long history, its importance as a major form in Iranian music today, and its extensive development during the twentieth century when the influence of Western music is so strong, the tasnif in itself could be the subject of an extensive treatise. Its discussion here, however, will be limited to its form as it relates to the radif and to a brief discussion of performance practices.

Each tasnif is written in one of the twelve dastgah of Persian music. Aside from using the scale of the dastgah, the tasnif may also use melodic motives particular to that dastgah and may contain a modulation to the major gusheh of the dastgah. These characteristics are illustrated by the tasnif in Example 106. It is in the dastgah of Shur, with its tonic on a′ and a scale of A B♭ C D E♭ F G A. The opening section, mm. 1–18, is in the main tetrachord of Shur, A–D, with an auxiliary note G, and stresses the note A as in the daramad of Shur. The following section, mm. 19–29, which stresses the third scale degree, C, and its dominant, G, is a reference to the gusheh Rohab. A movement to Shahnaz on the fourth degree, mm. 30–35, precedes a second mention of Rohab, mm. 36–44. The high point of the tasnif occurs in the two repeated sections, mm. 45–50 and mm. 51–56, which refer to the gusheh of Hosseini on the eighth degree. Closing the tasnif is the descent back to the original tetrachord of Shur, mm. 57–64.

EXAMPLE 106.   Payan, *DT*, p. 12

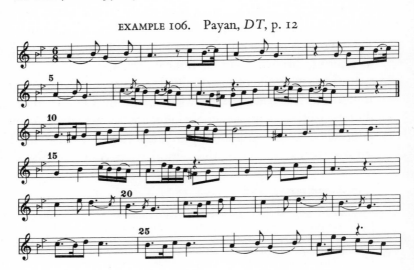

Many tasnif-ha written during the last twenty-five years do not contain this close relation to the radif. They are in the major or minor modes and contain no melodic or modulatory references to a dastgah. Thus, the claim that the tasnif is a "miniature dastgah" or that the listener can get a reduced picture of the dastgah from listening to a tasnif is somewhat exaggerated.[20]

Large numbers of tasnif-ha have been published and are now obtainable in Tehran. Among the collections of tasnif-ha is a large volume containing fifty ballads by one of the most prolific modern tasnif writers, Amir Jahed.[21] Tasnif-ha are regularly printed in the issues of the radio station's magazine [22] and in the periodical *Muzik-e Iran*. The ability to read musical notation, however, is not yet universal among Iranian musicians, and many singers still learn tasnif-ha by rote.

When notated, the tasnif appears only in melodic outline.

---

20. Khatchi, *Der Dastgah*, p. 125. His example does indeed show extraordinary correspondence with the unmeasured avaz melody taken from the radif. But his example was taken from an atypical source: a suite by Mussa Maʿruffi, *Avaz-e Dashti, Daftar-e Aval* (Tehran, 1948).

21. *Divan Amir Jahed* (Tehran, 1926).

22. *Majaleh-ye Musiqi-ye Radio Iran* (1957 ff).

As in the music of the radif, the singer is expected to embellish the tasnif liberally, creating an individual nuance or expression (halat). Singers are judged favorably when they are able to add long and profuse embellishments to a melody. The early notated tasnif-ha also contained no notated part for the instrumentalist, since he was expected to improvise his part as in the accompaniment of avaz in the radif.

During the late twenties and thirties, the composer and theorist Ali Naqi Vaziri began the practice of adding to the tasnif a composed instrumental introduction and several orchestral ritornelli. In the tasnif-ha written today, after every verse or two is a section for instruments. A further development that occurred about this time was the harmonizing of tasnif-ha. It is now common practice for the tasnif-ha used on radio and television to be harmonized and scored for orchestra. See Example 107.

The tasnif may be sung by itself or may be incorporated into a suite that uses the other composed forms, pish-daramad and reng,

EXAMPLE 107.   The opening of the tasnif Nargas-e Mast, Khaleqi (arrangement)

or it may be performed before and after a portion of avaz from the radif. Within classical Persian music, the tasnif is presently the form where the greatest experimentation is occurring. A development with much potential is the instrumental tasnif, a piece for solo instrumentalist and drummer based on a vocal tasnif. These compositions are now widely played and, with their attractive rhythms and melody, are rapidly displacing the classical radif. Just as instrumental transcriptions of vocal pieces heralded the development of independent instrumental music in the West, the instrumental tasnif appears to be having the same function in Persia. Example 108 presents a tasnif for the santur in the dastgah of Chahargah.

EXAMPLE 108. The opening of an instrumental tasnif in Chahargah

The Pish-daramad. This genre of composition, the newest of the three major forms, is truly a landmark in the history of Persian music. As noted, the Islamic attitudes toward music sufficiently discouraged all public concerts in Persia from the seventh century to the twentieth. A further discouragement in the late nineteenth century was the government prohibition against public gatherings for any purpose. In 1906, with the granting of the Persian constitution, restrictions on public gatherings were relaxed. Musicians were quick to seize their opportunity to come out in the open, and a public concert was finally held: perhaps to compensate for the millennia-long dearth of public concerts, it lasted twenty-four hours! This famous concert was held in a garden on the outskirts of the city, on a national holiday—the birthday of the first Imam Ali—and both music and meals were provided for participants. The sponsors were a Dervish order, the Okhovat Society, a group still in existence today.[23] No one remembers the exact number of musicians taking part in this momentous gathering, but apparently there were too many players for any sort of collective improvisation. In order that all might perform together for a gala overture, a new form was invented by the composer Darvish Khan (d. 1926). Called the pish-daramad (before the daramad), this form far outlasted the public concerts, which were discontinued after a few years when the government again grew sensitive to large gatherings.

As its name implies, the pish-daramad served as an introduction to the daramad, the prelude of a dastgah performance. It is a rhythmic composition for instruments, at first neither notated nor harmonized. Similar to the early tasnif, the pish-daramad is in one of the twelve dastgah and often contains melodic fragments of that dastgah.[24] Many collections of these pieces are available in published editions.[25] In Example 109, a pish-daramad from the

23. The Okhovat Society appears to be a bit tamer now. When I visited a meeting in 1965, instead of music there was a long lecture on morality.

24. An analysis of a pish-daramad is found in Khatchi, *Der Dastgah*, pp. 118–119. Its structural resemblance to an unmeasured avaz from the same dastgah is demonstrated.

25. *Hijdah Qateh-ye Pish-Daramad*, 3d ed., Lutfollah Moqadam Payan (Tehran, 1956); *Bist o Panj Qateh-ye Zarbi*, ed. Lutfollah Moqadam Payan (Tehran, 1948). The latter volume contains tasnif-ha, pish-daramad-ha, and reng-ha.

dastgah of Mahur, there is a modulation to the gusheh of Delkash in mm. 33–58 where the accidentals B-koron and C-natural are added.

EXAMPLE 109. Payan, *Hijdah Qateh-ye Pish Daramad*, p. 18

The Reng. Completing the survey of composed Persian music is a dance form, the reng.[26] Like the tasnif and unlike the pish-daramad, the reng appears to have been a well established form early in the history of the present radif, and unlike both other forms, some traditional reng-ha are included in the radif. One of the first sources for the radif, that of Mirza Abdullah given by Hedayat in *Madjma al Advar*, lists several reng-ha appropriate to each dastgah.[27] Recent versions of the radif also contain reng-ha as the closing piece of the dastgah.

The reng is usually in triple meter with a prominent dotted rhythm.[28] When used as part of the radif, at the closing portion of a dastgah, the reng may be improvised, since it is not difficult to play melodies characteristic of the dastgah in the rhythm of a reng. These pieces also occur as composed, nonimprovised forms outside of the radif. Many have been notated and exist in published collections.[29] Examples 110–111 contains a reng in Bayat-e Tork by Saba and one in Dashti by Maʿruffi.

EXAMPLE 110. The opening of a reng in Bayat-e Tork. Khaleqi, *Majaleh-ye Chang*, no. 1, p. 9

26. Dancing was a highly favored court entertainment and a typical subject for wall paintings and miniatures. Besides iconographic evidence, little has been reported regarding the actual dancing and the music that accompanied it. See Mejid Rezvani, *Le théâtre et la danse en Iran* (Paris, 1963).

27. Khatchi, *Der Dastgah*, pp. 16–23.

28. The subject of rhythm used for the reng-ha is treated by Hormoz Farhat in *Majaleh-ye Musiqi* 25.

29. Payan, *Bist o Panj Qateh-ye Zarbi*; Mohammad Baharlu, *Ketab-e Chaharom-e Musiqi-ye Irani* (Tehran, 1958). The radif of Mussa Maʿruffi in *MTI* contains several reng-ha.

EXAMPLE III. The opening of a reng in Dashti. Khaleqi, *Majaleh-ye Chang*, no. 1, p. 9

The Combination of Improvised and Nonimprovised Forms

A typical form for traditional Persian art music is a four-movement suite consisting of pish-daramad, avaz (the portion from the radif), tasnif, and reng. In these suites, the four movements are from the same dastgah and often show similarities in their melodies. A few suites have been written by individual composers and published, but most are simply put together from separate existing movements.[30] Within the last five years, however, the use of the pish-daramad and reng in this form have declined in popularity. Now a combination of tasnif and avaz is customarily performed, the orchestral introduction to the tasnif serving in place of the pish-daramad. A piece called tarana (song or trill), used for radio programs of Persian music, may be broken down as follows:

30. One of these is that of Maʿruffi, *Avaz-e Dashti*. He has also written a suite in the dastgah of chahargah.

1. Orchestral introduction to the tasnif.
2. Verses of the tasnif with orchestral ritornelli between them.
3. Orchestral conclusion of the tasnif (which might be the same as the introduction).
4. A part of the radif with perhaps an instrumental solo between sections of vocal avaz.
5. Repeat of the orchestral introduction to the tasnif or part of the tasnif.

The combination of improvised and nonimprovised forms is not restricted to vocal and orchestral pieces but may also be used for solo instrumental performances. Younger players, especially when performing for large audiences or for the mass media, devote a large part of their performance to composed pieces of a lighter, more easily understood style. As the sections of pish-daramad, tasnif, chahar-mezrab, and so forth increase in length, so do the sections of avaz between them get correspondingly shorter. This type of performance, often called majlesi (for a large gathering), is a response to more popular taste of the new Iranian audiences, for it favors the increase in familiarity produced by composed pieces, the interest in virtuoso display pieces such as chahar mezrab, and, finally, a desire for a simpler melodic style.[31]

Future observers may find that this trend toward measured and composed pieces is part of an important style shift in Persian classical music. During the last thirty years, with the introduction of radio and television in Iran, the audience for this music has changed radically, and composers are changing styles that were suitable for traditional elite gatherings. Thus, classical Persian music appears to be moving away from an unmeasured music created by the technique of improvisation to a measured one that is largely composed.

31. Examples of this trend are ample in the transcriptions by Eckart Wilkins in *Künstler und Amateure im persischen Santurspiel* (Regensburg, 1967).

6   Persian Musical Instruments

Peoples of the Middle East, with their special fondness for musical artifacts and skill in creating them, have had a wide variety of instruments since ancient times. These constitute an important study in themselves, both for their long history and for their cross influences throughout various Middle Eastern cultures. An equally significant aspect of Middle Eastern organology for the Western scholar is the relationship between these instruments and those of Europe. It is generally recognized that most European musical instruments have their origin in Asia. Indeed, Curt Sachs, in his *History of Musical Instruments*, goes so far as to say that "at the beginning of modern times, Europe possessed almost exclusively instruments of Near Eastern descent, some of them Byzantine but most of them Islamic."[1]

A study of musical instruments has certain advantages over a study of the music itself, for the sources are generally more plentiful than for any other aspect of music. Instruments are tangible artifacts: they can either be found and examined at first hand, or they can be studied from carvings, sculptures, or drawings contemporary with the period in which they were used. In both cases, instruments can be described with relative precision, and they are thus more accessible historically than the music played on them. For the ancient period, archaeological evidence is available; and, iconographical sources and a number of detailed theoretical treatises give information on instruments in the medieval and modern periods.

1. New York, 1940, p. 246.

When tracing the instruments used for Persian music to their origins and examining the source material, one is again impressed by the length of Persia's history. Archaeological evidence comes down to us even from the pre-Achaemenid period, that is, before the sixth century B.C. From the middle of the second millenium B.C. there are gold and silver objects believed to be signal horns.[2] From the eighth century B.C., a beautifully preserved terra-cotta figurine showing a tambur player was found at Susa, and from the seventh century, there is an Elamite relief of three musicians, located in southwest Iran near the town of Masjed-e Suleyman.[3] And from the Achaemenid period survives a trumpet found at Persepolis that is believed to have been used in the court of Artaxerxes III (d. 338 B.C.).[4]

In the next major Persian dynasty, the Sassanian (third to seventh centuries A.D.), iconographical sources for musical instruments become more plentiful. The most famous source is the series of rock carvings at Taq-i Bustan, near the city of Kermanshah. Located inside a shallow cave, these carvings have been quite well preserved, and today one can see numerous scenes of hunters stalking wild boars to the rather incongruous accompaniment of boatloads of musicians. Numerous gold and silver plates surviving from this period further illustrate several kinds of musical instruments.

During the early Islamic period in Persia there are virtually no representations of instruments. Not only did Islam frown upon music and especially musical instruments, but it took an equally strong position against the representation of the human figure in painting and in sculpture. We are compensated for this lack of iconographical evidence, however, by various descriptions of instruments, for example, those in the treatises of al-Farabi, Ibn Sina and Safi al-Din. The most complete is that of al-Farabi which comprises one entire book of his treatise *Kitab al Kabir*.[5]

2. Erich F. Schmidt, *Excavations at Tepe Hissar* (Philadelphia, 1937), pp. 209–210. This reference was shown me by Dr. T. C. Young, Jr.

3. Arthur U. Pope and Phyllis Ackerman, *A Survey of Persian Art*, 6 vols. (London, 1939), plate 74; L. Vandenberghe, "Les reliefes elamites de Malamir," *Iranica Antiqua* 3 (1963).

4. This trumpet, three feet long with a bell twenty-four inches in diameter, was discovered in 1957 and is now in the museum at the site of Persepolis.

5. *MA*, I, 164–322.

Scenes from the rock carvings at Taq-i Bustan showing boatloads of harpists.

A brass ewer from the thirteenth century showing players of the drum, tambourine, and flute.

Also of great value for the study of instruments is the Persian treatise *Kanz al Tuhaf*, probably written during the fourteenth century.[6]

Abundant iconography appears once again in the great period of Persian miniatures, starting in the fourteenth century and reaching its height in the sixteenth and seventeenth; and the group of wall murals in the palace of Chehel Sotun in Esfahan presents a useful catalog of instruments played during the Safavid period. Descriptions of instruments in Persia written by European travelers or historians, first appearing in antiquity, began to be written again in the seventeenth century.[7] Finally, studies of musical instruments by European musicologists date from the mid-nineteenth century. Usually quite detailed, they have been of considerable importance in the present study.[8]

Here we shall concentrate on the historical development and present state of the six major instruments used for the performance of classical music in Iran: two plucked pandores, the tar and the sehtar, from the family of long-necked lutes; a bowed string instrument, the kamanchay; a struck zither or dulcimer, the santur; a vertical flute, the nay; and a small drum, the tombak. At the time of this writing, the tar, sehtar, santur, and tombak are widely used throughout Iran, both in Tehran and the provincial cities. It does not appear that they are rapidly being superseded by Western instruments. The kamanchay, on the other hand, has been replaced almost completely in Tehran by the violin, although it is still played in the provinces. The same is true of the nay, which, by professional musicians, is being replaced by the Western transverse flute.

In addition to these six instruments, others are of special interest. Folk music instruments are often unchanged from medieval times; indeed, some of the instruments used in Iranian villages today may be traced back to antiquity. Another class of Persian instruments to be considered are those that are no longer widely

---

6. This treatise appears in French in *LavE*, p. 3071. See also Henry G. Farmer, *Sources of Arabian Music*, rev. ed. (Leiden, 1965), pp. 54–55.

7. The works of Chardin, le Brun, Thevenot, Advielle, and Sherley are listed in the bibliography.

8. Works by Sachs and Lavignac have been cited. Also of interest are the studies by R. G. Kiesewetter and J. P. N. Land.

A page from the sixteenth-century *Khamza* of Nizami showing court musicians playing the duff and ʿud.

A page from the sixteenth-century *Khamza* showing musicians at the lower left playing the duff and chang, at the lower right, the kamanchay and nay.

played but are presently being revived by the Ministry of Culture:. the ᶜud (lute), qanun (psaltery), and qaychek (viol). Finally, there are the chang (harp) and the rebab (viol), which have now disappeared from Persia but have considerable historical significance.

INSTRUMENTS USED FOR ART MUSIC

The Tar

The most widely used plucked stringed instrument in Iran today is the tar (string, or chord). Although its name is old, the instrument itself appears to be relatively new. The tar is not mentioned by any of the medieval writers; neither is it portrayed in the miniatures of the sixteenth or seventeenth centuries. Furthermore, it is conspicuously absent from the chief iconographic source of the Safavid period (sixteenth to eighteenth centuries), the wall paintings of musicians on the palace of Chehel Sotun. Persian theorists usually date the appearance of the tar in Iran with the Qajar period (late eighteenth to twentieth centuries), when it begins to be depicted in miniatures and photographs.

The origin of this uniquely shaped, double-bellied instrument has not yet been established. Its unusual form and possible relation to the European guitar—which has a more refined version of the same general shape and a relation in name—awaken one's interest. Two hypotheses seem applicable here. One is that the tar evolved sometime during the seventeenth and eighteenth centuries from other Iranian instruments. Its long neck and system of frets resemble the sehtar, an instrument with a long history in Iran. The sehtar, however, does not possess either of the distinctive features of the tar, the skin membrane or the double belly. These two characteristics are found in another old Iranian instrument, the gaycheck, which, however, has a short neck and is bowed. A second hypothesis is that it came directly from the Caucasus, where a similar instrument may be found today.[9]

The double-bellied body of the tar is made of mulberry wood carved in two sections, cutting the body in half from front to

9. R. Khaleqi, in conversation.

back. These sections are joined by a vertical seam glued around the back and bottom of the instrument. The long neck is also glued to the body. A standard tar is 95 cm. in length, 25 cm. across the widest part and 20 cm. deep, with a neck of 60 cm. It is a heavy instrument, and in order to support it on the knee, some players use a small footrest that raises the leg to a comfortable position.

The face of the tar is a sheepskin membrane in two separate sections, the lower one about one and one-half times larger than the upper. The bridge supporting the strings is attached directly to the lower membrane, and since the membrane is affected by changes in temperature and humidity, the tuning of the tar is likely to be quite delicate. In Iran, where the climate is temperate and extremely dry, this is less of a problem, and the membrane can be fairly thin. Weather conditions in the Caucasus, however, are not so favorable, and a thicker membrane must be used.

The six strings of the tar are made of metal, five of steel and one, the lowest, of brass. They are tuned in pairs, usually c c′, g g, and c′ c′. According to Khaleqi, the tar had only five strings this century, when the musician Darvish Khan added the c′, beside the lowest c. The above tuning is standard for the instrument, but other special tunings are customarily used for different dastgah-ha. For example, those tunings for the tar given in one radif by Mussa Maʿruffi, are as follows:

c	c′	g g	c′ c′		for Mahur and Chahargah
f	c′	g g	c′ c′		for Shur and Abu Ata
d	d′	g g	c′ c′		for Afshari, Dashti, Nava, Homayun, and Esfahan
eʰ	eʰ	g g	c′ c′		for Sehgah
c	c′	f f	c′ c′		for Bayat-e Tork and Rast Panjgah

The standard number of frets on the tar is twenty-six. They are made of gut and are movable. Between each two whole-tone frets are two other frets, one for the flatted form of the higher note and one for its koron, or three-quarter-tone form. There is no fret between the half steps E–F and B–C. The range of the tar is normally from c to g″. An exception is the tar designed by Ali

Musicians posing at the shop of an instrument maker (early twentieth century).
Note the carved bodies of several tar in the foreground and a soon-to-be-carved
tree trunk.

Naqi Vaziri, the neck of which extends further down onto the
body of the instrument. This lower part of the neck contains
six extra frets, extending its range one tetrachord higher, that is,
from g″ to c‴.

The tar is plucked with a small metal plectrum inserted into a
gum ball held between the thumb and index finger. There are
two strokes with this plectrum: the downstroke is called rast
(right); the upstroke, chap (left). (This terminology is reversed
on the sehtar, which uses the index finger as a plectrum. Here the
upstroke is stronger and is called rast; the downstroke is chap.)

The first book of Iranian music to be printed in Western
notation was an instruction manual for the tar by Ali Naqi
Vaziri.[10] *Dastur-e Tar* contains a wide variety of pieces, including
selections from the radif and arrangements of Western classical
pieces for two tar. In 1951, Mr. Khaleqi edited a number of tar
instruction books for use in the Conservatory of National Music.
These contain only Iranian music and are still in use. A published
edition of the complete radif for tar is the radif of Mussa Maʿruffi,[11]

10. *Dastur-e Tar* (Berlin, 1913).
11. *MTI*.

Hossein Gholi, brother of Mirza Abdullah and master of the tar.

and the radif of Abol Hassan Saba, already published for violin and for santur, is in the process of being published for the tar.

There have been many eminent players of the tar during the last century.[12] The family of Ali Akbar Farhani, court musician to Nasir ed din Shah, has produced three generations of string players who were, in turn, the chief musicians of their time.[13] Mirza Abdullah, who is credited with the modern classification of the radif, was the son of Ali Akbar, as was Hossein Gholi, another noted teacher. The son of Hossein Gholi, Shahnazi, living today, is one of the foremost tar players in Iran, while the son of Mirza Abdullah, Ahmad Ebadi, is the leading sehtar player.

At present the tar is used both as a solo instrument and to accompany singers. It is also used in orchestras of native instruments. Special pieces have also been written for large ensembles of tar-ha, one for fourteen tar. The instrument is readily accessible in the music shops, costing generally from ten to one hundred dollars.

12. Because the placement of frets and the notation system for the sehtar are similar to those of the tar, many of these players were masters of both instruments but are known as tar virtuosi.

13. Ali Akbar's playing was described by Count Gobineau in *Trois ans en Asie* (Paris, 1859), II, 212.

The Sehtar

The instruction manuals and transcriptions of the radif made for the tar can also be used for the smaller Persian instrument, the sehtar, since the number of frets and the tuning are identical for both. Contrary to the literal meaning of its name, which is "three strings," the modern sehtar has four, two of steel and two of brass, tuned to c, c', g, and c'. The range is the same as that of the tar, c to g".

Although the systems of frets and notation are similar for the tar and the sehtar, the sehtar is an independent instrument, not simply a smaller tar. In contrast to the parchment-covered, double-bellied tar, the sehtar has a pear-shaped body made entirely of wood and is of much lighter construction.[14] There are a number of small holes carved in the face and sides of the belly to increase the resonance. An average sehtar is 85 cm. long, 20 cm. wide, and 15 cm. deep. The player uses no plectrum, but instead strikes the strings with the nail of his right index finger, which he has let grow long.

Since the sehtar is much more delicate than the tar, its sound is correspondingly softer. Like the Western clavichord, the tone of the sehtar does not carry from one room to the next.[15] Hence it can be played in secret and is ideally suited to Persia, where playing an instrument was traditionally subject to disapproval. Furthermore, to be appreciated, it must be played before a gathering that is both small and quiet. Thus the sehtar is ideal for the intimate settings characteristic of Persian art music, and for this reason it is often considered the most typical Persian instrument.

Of all the stringed instruments used today in Iran, the sehtar has the longest history. Its predecessors, belonging to the pandore family, were depicted in Middle Eastern bas reliefs during the second millenium B.C.[16] From Iran, an especially clear example

14. Sehtar-ha are also constructed with a flat body for convenience when traveling.

15. Another similarity to the clavichord is the use of bebung, or vibrato. On the sehtar it is produced by vibrating the neck of the instrument, a technique used by all players. This observation was made by Curt Sachs, *The History of Musical Instruments* (New York, 1940), p. 255.

16. Henry G. Farmer, "An Early Greek Pandore," *Oriental Studies, Mainly Musical* (London, 1953), p. 61.

Ahmad Ebadi, the leading master of the sehtar in Iran today and the son of Mirza Abdullah.

of the ancient pandore is the eighth century B.C. terra-cotta figure of a man plucking a long-necked stringed instrument that was found at Susa and is now in the Louvre.[17] During the Achaemenid and Sassanian periods, there is no source material for the pandore. It reappears as the tambur during the early Islamic period, having grown in importance along with the lute. The Islamic theorists al-Farabi and Safi al-Din include the tambur in their discussion of instruments and distinguish between the

17. Henry G. Farmer, "Outline History of Music and Music Theory," in Pope and Ackerman, *Survey of Persian Art*, p. 2784.

tambur of Baghdad and that of Khorassan, the northeastern province of Iran.[18] Later, during the great period of Persian miniature painting, the tambur or sehtar was a favorite subject.[19]

The sehtar seems to have relinquished its popularity to the tar during the Qajar period (eighteenth to twentieth centuries), and it does not often appear in Qajar drawings and paintings. It is likely that then, as now, the musicians famous as tar players, for example, the ladies Mina and Zohreh and the famous Ali Akbar, also played the sehtar but did not specialize in it. It is significant that in his historical study of twentieth-century Iranian music Khaleqi does not devote a separate chapter to the sehtar as he does for all other instruments.

Because its tone is so delicate, the sehtar is always used as a solo instrument. It is not included in orchestras of native instruments, nor is it frequently used to accompany a singer. In the present generation of players, new impetus has been given to the instrument by the son of Mirza Abdullah, Ahmad Ebadi. He has specialized in playing the sehtar rather than the tar and is considered by many Iranians to be the finest musician living today. With the use of mass media, the sehtar has lost its insularity, and Ebadi can be heard by a wide public on Radio Iran.

The Nay

The simplest and perhaps the oldest instrument used for the performance of Persian classical music is the nay. This vertical flute can be traced back to prehistoric times in the Middle East. In fact, Sachs mentions one from the fourth millennium B.C. recorded on a slate from Hieraconpolis.[20] Instruments like the nay can be found throughout the Middle East and Asia.

The nay is made of a long piece of cane, often decorated with

---

18. *MA*, I, 218–261; III, 366–369. Both tamburs were important for their systems of tuning. The two strings of the tambur of Baghdad were divided into forty parts with frets at points 35 to 39. The intervals between frets were in the range of a quarter tone. The tambur of Khorassan, on the other hand, was fretted in units of limma, limma, and comma. According to Owen Wright, the scale produced on this tambur was second in popularity "only to that of the lute, and it probably occasioned some of the changes that took place in the Arabian Scale." "Ibn al-Munajjim and the Early Arabian Modes," *The Galpin Society Journal* 19 (April 1966), p. 42.

19. Pope and Ackerman, *Survey of Persian Art*, plates 889, 915-b, and 792-b.

20. Sachs, *History of Musical Instruments*, p. 90.

Nahib Esdolleh, a famous player of the nay.

figures and wound in several places with cord or plastic for decoration and for strength. Fifty to sixty centimeters long, it often has a metal mouthpiece that is simply an extension of the cane. Near the lower end are six finger holes on the front and generally one hole in the back. The player holds his instrument slanting downwards, blowing across the upper edge. An unusual feature of the nay is the two different mouth positions. To blow the tones of the lower register, the player holds the instrument against one side of his nearly closed lips. The notes of the upper register are produced by inserting the end of the instrument between the two upper front teeth with the player's upper lip entirely covering the end of the mouthpiece. (By fortunate coincidence, or as a result of extensive practicing, most nay players have a space between their upper front teeth.)

Because the construction of the nay is still so simple—it is only a piece of cane or reed with holes bored into it—this instrument is difficult to play well. A pure tone, without excessive breathiness, is achieved only rarely; thus, professional players are correspondingly few. The leading nay player in Iran today is the elderly musician from Esfahan, Kassayi, who may be heard on the radio. The nay is, of course, one of the most important folk instruments, typically played by shepherds. In some of the provinces of Iran, a shorter transverse flute may be used instead of the long vertical one.

The nay holds a special place in the music of the Sufis. It is a "symbol of the spirit that lifts man's soul to the divine principle,"[21] and the most important Sufi poem, the *Masnavi* by Jalal ed Din Rumi, opens with an invocation to listen to the nay:

> Hearken to this Reed forlorn,
> Breathing, even since 'twas torn
> From its rushy bed, a strain
> Of impassioned love and pain.
>
> "The secret of my song, though near,
> None can see and none can hear
> Oh, for a friend to know the sign,
> And mingle all his soul with mine."
>
> " 'Tis the flame of Love that fired me,
> 'Tis the wine of Love inspired me.
> Wouldst thou learn how lovers bleed,
> Hearken, hearken to the Reed!"[22]

The Santur

This important Persian instrument belongs to the category of zithers, "string instruments which have no neck or yoke, whose strings are usually open, not stopped, and whose resonating body can be a board, box, stick or tube."[23] In the class of board zithers are both psalteries and dulcimers, as well as the Western keyboard instruments. The psaltery usually has strings of gut, silk, or nylon, and the strings are plucked. The dulcimer, on the other hand, has metal strings that are struck with plectra.

Both kinds of zither, psalteries and dulcimers, are found in Persia. The Iranian psaltery or plucked zither is the qanun, an instrument now rarely used in Iran, but still extremely important

---

21. Jules Rouanet, "La musique arabe," in *LavE*, p. 2791 (my translation).
22. Reynold A. Nicholson, *Rumi, Poet and Mystic* (London, 1950), p. 31.
23. Sachs, *History of Musical Instruments*, pp. 463–464.

in the Arab countries.[24] The dulcimer, or santur, on the other hand, is extremely popular in Iran, but it has almost completely disappeared from the Arab countries.

In contrast to most Middle Eastern musical instruments, neither type of zither can be traced to antiquity.[25] The ancient stringed instrument closest to the zither family—that is, with no neck and unstopped strings—was the harp. One may hypothesize that the zither developed from the harp, perhaps late in the first millennium A.D., but it is not mentioned in literature or depicted iconographically until several centuries later. The name *santur* first appears in a poem that describes various kinds of birds who play musical instruments, by an eleventh-century Persian, Manucheri.[26] The instrument itself, however, was not depicted until the thirteenth-century drawing from the *Kitab al-Adwar* of Safi al-Din (d. 1294). Here the zither is rectangular and is called al-nuzha.[27] In the fourteenth-century Persian treatise *Kanz al Tuhaf*, the nuzha is again mentioned and credited to Safi al-Din.[28] The wall paintings of Chehel Sotun, the "catalog" of Safavid musical instruments, also depict the santur, and it is later found in paintings and photographs from the Qajar period. In the twentieth century, the santur has gained great popularity, and now it is one of the major instruments in Persia.

European countries during the medieval period possessed both plucked and struck zithers, probably of Middle Eastern origin. The dulcimer appears frequently in eighteenth-century European drawings played by elegantly costumed gentlemen and ladies.[29]

24. See p. 181 below.

25. Sachs states that zithers did not exist in Egypt or Assyria and that the psaltery mentioned in the *Bible* indicates a harp. *History of Musical Instruments*, pp. 116–117.

26. This use of the word santur is suggested in *SMI*, p. 168. Professor Mujtaba Minovi offers the hypothesis that this word could also be *shaypour*, meaning "trumpet," and not *santour*. In several manuscripts of the Manucheri poem, the word is written as shaypour, for example, in *The Divan of Ostod Manucheri Damghani*, Mohammad Dabirsi'aghi, ed. (Tehran, 1936), p. 3, n. 4. Confusion arises in this case because the basic shape of both words is the same. They differ only in the addition of dots above and below the letters. In older manuscripts the dots were often omitted, so it is impossible to tell which word was intended by calligraphy alone.

27. Frontispiece to Henry G. Farmer's "Arabic Musical Manuscripts in the Bodleian Library," *JRAS* 4 (1925).

28. *LavE*, p. 3072.

29. Alexandre Buchner, *Musical Instruments Through the Ages* (London, 1956), plates 212 and 213. Filippo Bonanni, *The Showcase of Musical Instruments* [reprint, *Gabinetto Armonico*, Rome, 1723] (New York, 1964), plate 64. The Persian origin of the European dulcimer is also mentioned by Anthony Baines in *Musical Instruments Through the Ages* (London, 1961), pp. 206–207.

Whether or not the dulcimer—whose strings are beaten with wooden hammers, often covered with felt—inspired the first makers of the piano is open to speculation. Curt Sachs claims a connection between the dulcimer and the piano through the popular dulcimer player Pantaleon Hebenstreit, who toured Europe around 1700 displaying the advantages of this reputedly "primitive" instrument.[30] The dulcimer is still found in Europe as a folk instrument, especially in the southeast; it is also played in some southern regions of the United States.[31]

The Iranian struck zither, the santur, is a shallow box in the form of a regular trapezoid. Inside the box are wooden props which strengthen the instrument and contribute to the resonance, and the top surface is pierced with two small rosettes. There are seventy-two strings, arranged in groups of four, that is, for each note there are four strings of identical pitch and thus eighteen four-string groups (see Figure 4). The strings, strung from left to right, are tightened by means of metal pegs inserted directly into the right-hand side of the box. Each group of four strings is supported by a small wooden bridge. The bridges of the santur are cleverly arranged to produce the rather sizeable range of three octaves on a fairly small playing surface. There are two sets of nine strings—one set of brass, the other of steel—strung alternately from top to bottom. The notes of the lowest octave, e to f′, are played on the brass strings whose bridges are set along the far right side, thus providing a long length of string and a low pitch. The notes of the two higher octaves, e′ to f″ and e″ to f‴, are played on the steel strings whose bridges along the left side are placed so as to divide the string into two sections, or short and medium lengths for the high and the middle ranges respectively. Thus, each group of steel strings and the adjacent brass strings give three notes: from left to right, e″, e′, and e. The note e‴ can be played on the extreme right of the brass strings, but this is not usual.

As the santur is presently tuned in Tehran, there is only one

---

30. Sachs, *History of Musical Instruments*, p. 391. According to Willi Apel, however, the very earliest inventor of the pianoforte mechanism, Bartolomo Christofori, did not hear Hebenstreit. *Harvard Dictionary of Music* (Cambridge, 1944), s.v. Pianoforte.

31. In Russia, the gusli is a related instrument, as is the tzimbalon in Hungary. Close resemblances are found in the santur-ha of Turkey, modern Greece, and Kashmir.

The santur virtuoso Hossein Malek. His instrument is set into a platform with dampers on either side that are controlled by a pedal.

group of strings for each of the seven notes of the octave, with the exception of E and F, which have duplicate strings.[32] A single note in any given register, therefore, can have only one value, that is, the note G can be tuned to G-natural, G-flat, G-sharp, or either of the microintervals, G-koron or G-sori, but not to more than one of these at the same time. If the player requires both a G-natural and a G-koron in the same piece, he must sound one of them in a different register.[33] This limitation does not usually present great difficulties in traditional Persian art music, where the number of accidentals in a single perform-ance is relatively small.[34] But for performances of Western music,

32. Santur players use slightly different tunings in different regions of Iran. In Shiraz, for example, the lowest string is often c rather than e.

33. Although the pegs that support the strings are movable, they cannot be repositioned with ease, and it is not customary to move them while playing. Single strings in the qanun, on the other hand, can easily be adjusted while playing.

34. Occasionally one finds melodic lines with abrupt changes of register to accommo-date an accidental, as in Example 6, chapter 2.

or Persian music written in a Western style, the ordinary santur is inadequate. Recently a chromatic santur was developed with five extra string groups in each octave. These give the same notes as the five black notes on the piano. The chromatic santur is used in Iranian orchestras that perform Western-style music.

A typical santur measures 35 cm. and 90 cm. for the two horizontal sides of the trapezoid, 25 cm. across, and 5 cm. deep. There are smaller instruments whose overall pitch is one or two notes higher, and also a larger variety with an added lower octave. A fair instrument may be purchased in Tehran for about twenty-five dollars, and there are excellent santurs available for several hundred dollars.

The striking hammers used for the santur, mezrab-ha (plectra), are supple wooden sticks made of mulberry or walnut, about 20 cm. long, whose shape varies slightly from maker to maker. Many contemporary santur players cover the ends of their mezrab-ha with felt, cotton batting, or rubber to produce a softer, more subtle sound. Covered mezrab-ha give a tone close to that of the piano, instead of the brilliant metallic tone produced by bare wooden plectra. The use of covered mezrab-ha is significant in the light of traditional musical practice in Iran. Because musical gatherings are customarily small, instruments of delicate timbre were cultivated, the soft-voiced sehtar being the best example. The one native chamber music instrument capable of producing a rather loud tone was the santur. This has now been subdued to conform to the prevailing dynamic level of Persian instruments and to make possible its inclusion in the newly popular orchestras of native instruments.

Most of the present generation of santur players in Tehran were trained by the venerated master Abol Hassan Saba (d. 1957), whose radif for santur is now published in four volumes.[35] Other santur virtuosi in Tehran are Faramarz Payvar and Hossein Saba (d. 1959), both of whom have written instruction manuals,[36] and Hossein Malek and Mohammed Heydari.

---

35. *Durey-e Aval-e, Dovom-e, Sevom-e*, 4 vols (Tehran, 1958–1960).
36. *Chaharom-e Santur*; Faramarz Payvar, *Dastur-e Santur* (Tehran, 1957); Hossein Saba, *Khod Amuz, Santur* (Tehran, 1955).

The Kamanchay

The Persian member of that large family of bowed string instruments found throughout the Middle East is the kamanchay. This instrument is part of the generic class of spike fiddles, that is, those having a metal spike extending from the bottom of the sound chest, like the Western cello. The spike of the kamanchey is not sharp but is tipped with a flat metal plate which the player rests on his thigh, or on his calf when he is seated on the ground. The spike is attached to this plate in such a manner that the instrument can be rotated slightly while playing. A modern kamanchay has four strings, and whereas in Tehran it is tuned like the violin, provincial kamanchay-ha have fewer strings and different tunings. The body is a hemisphere made of wood, usually of wooden strips glued together, with a round face, covered with a sheepskin membrane. The neck, which has no frets, is glued to the body. The instrument is about the size of the Western viola. The top end of the neck and the body are often highly decorated.

One predecessor of the Iranian kamanchay is the qazak or ghaychek, an instrument still played in southeastern Persia.[37] Although the qazak was used in Persia in pre-Islamic times, there is no evidence showing that it was then bowed.[38] Another possible predecessor of the kamanchay is the rebab, a large class of bowed instruments found throughout the Arab countries. Farmer lists seven different forms of rebab that have rectangular, circular, boat-shaped, pear-shaped, or hemispherical bodies. Closest to the Persian kamanchay is the hemispherical rebab.[39] This instrument is described by al-Farabi in his tenth-century book of musical instruments, but he does not describe its exact shape or the shape of the bow.[40]

The name *kamanchay* comes from the Persian word for bow, *kaman*, *kamanchay* being the diminutive form. The word *kamanchay* was used as early as the twelfth century in a poem by Masud

37. Khaleqi, *SMI*, p. 59. See below, pp. 181–183.
38. Henry G. Farmer, *A History of Arabian Music to the Thirteenth Century* (London, 1929), pp. 155, 210. Also Werner Bachmann, *Die Anfänge des Streichinstrumentenspiels*, 2d ed. (Leipzig, 1964).
39. Henry G. Farmer, "Rabab" [sic], in *Encyclopedia of Islam* (Leiden, 1936).
40. *MA*, I, 277–285.

A Qajar-style painting of a kamanchay player (nineteenth century).
Victoria and Albert Museum. Crown Copyright.

An early photograph showing kamanchay players.

Sad Salman (d.ca. 1131),[41] even though two centuries later, in the *Kanz al Tuhaf*, the term *ghaychek* is still used.[42]

Frequently represented in Persian miniatures of the Safavid period, [43] the kamanchay is also included in the wall paintings of Chehel Sotun. Until that fateful day when the violin came to Iran, during the reign of Mozaffar ed Din Shah (1898–1907), the kamanchay was one of the principal instruments of Persian music. But from that time on, the days of the kamanchay were numbered: Iranian players soon discovered that they could produce a more delicate tone and play more difficult passages on the Western instrument than on the kamanchay. Today, while the instrument is still widely played in the provinces, there are few kamanchay players in Tehran. The violin, usurper of that major position once held by the kamanchay, is now used for

41. Khaleqi, *SMI*, p. 62.
42. *LavE*, p. 3071.
43. Pope and Ackerman, *Survey of Persian Art*, plate 909-b.

Persian art music, being as popular as the tar, sehtar, or santur, and more Persian music is published for violin than for any other instrument.

The Tombak

Performances of Persian art music now use the tombak (also dombak) or zarb as the chief percussion instrument. This is a small one-faced drum whose upper half is wider than the lower. Carved of a single block of wood, its body is hollow, open at the lower end and covered with a sheepskin membrane at the upper. Because this membrane is glued firmly onto the frame, gross differences in tuning cannot be obtained. To prepare the drum head for playing, musicians warm it over a stove or an electric heater. The frame of the tombak is usually of wood, but inexpensive instruments are now constructed of metal. An average tombak is 40 cm. high with a playing face 25 cm. in diameter.

A tombak player holds the drum diagonally across his lap with the wider section over his right thigh.[44] The tombak is not played with drumsticks, but with the fingers and palms of both hands. Persian drummers, who have developed an elaborate technique, are able to produce a great variety of different sounds on the single face. For example, the thick, dull sound, tom, comes from striking the center of the face with the whole hand; the sharp, dry sound, bak, is produced by striking the face near the rim. For a rhythm such as one two-and three four, the first beat is the "tom," played by the right hand striking the center; beats "two" and "three" are played by the fourth finger of the left hand snapped against the thumb then onto the face near the rim of the drum, and beats "-and" and "four" by the third finger of the right hand striking the edge of the face.

In recent years, as rhythmic music has become more favored in classical Persian music, the use of the tombak has increased.[45]

---

44. Street musicians, who also play the tombak, attach a cord to both ends and hang the drum across their shoulders.

45. Khaleqi describes rhythmic music as if it were quite a recent innovation that Persians had to be urged to approve. He also states that Persians did not appreciate the skill of their tombak players, although visitors to Iran were amazed at what could be played on such a simple instrument. *SMI*, pp. 399–405.

A Qajar-style painting of a tombak player (nineteenth century).
Victoria and Albert Museum. Crown Copyright.

A virtuoso drummer of Iran, Hossein Tehrani.

Today instrumentalists seldom play without drum accompaniment, and younger players learn the tombak as a second instrument in order to accompany each other. The popularity of the tombak may also be due to the presence of a virtuoso player in Tehran. For the past twenty-five years, Hossein Tehrani has fascinated listeners with his virtuosity, and he has even been sent to perform in Europe by the Iranian government. A great number of students have been trained by Tehrani, and they now imitate many of his playing mannerisms, such as the scraping of a ring worn on the index finger along the ridged length of the drum to produce a humorous grating sound.

That the present tombak may be of recent origin is suggested by its absence from all iconographic sources until the Qajar period. The major percussion instrument for many centuries had been the daff, or tambourine; and it is this instrument that is presented in Persian miniatures and at Chehel Sotun.

FOLK INSTRUMENTS

Apart from the musical instruments used for Persian art music, there are many folk instruments found among the peasants and tribal people of Iran. The most widely used are the nay and the ghaychek, already discussed, and the surna (oboe), dahal (drum), daff and dayereh (tambourines), and the naghareh (kettledrum).

The surna, a shrill wind instrument, is the principal instrument for celebrations in Persian villages. In the cities, it is played for religious dramas (tazieh), for the tower music (naghareh khaneh), and also by wandering minstrels. The surna is part of a duo, the other half being a percussion instrument, usually the dahal.

Likely the predecessor of the oboe, the surna is a short conical instrument of about 35 cm. length, the bore being $2\frac{1}{2}$ cm. at the top and 7 cm. at the bell. The mouthpiece is a double reed 6 cm. long. In contrast to European oboe technique, where the player presses his lips around the upper end of the mouthpiece, the surna player inserts the entire reed into his mouth and presses his lips against a small metal circle perpendicular to the reed. With this mouth position and a special technique of breathing through his

A player of the surna.

nose, the player can blow continuously and need not stop the sound when taking a breath.

Instruments similar to the surna are found all over North Africa and Asia. This oboe originated in the Middle East, according to Sachs, and was carried to the Far East during the Islamic conquests.[46]

The music most often played on the surna consists of very short melodic motives of limited range, endlessly repeated. There is a stressing of the tonic note, and if two surna are playing, one will simply drone the tonic. Part of the appeal of this instrument is the hypnotic effect produced by the ceaseless repition of the bourdon note and the single phrase. Since the sound of the surna is loud and piercing, its shrill voice carries for many city blocks and for a greater distance in the open air.

The dahal, or shallow drum used to accompany the surna, is quite large, from 60 to 120 cm. in diameter, but only 15 or 20 cm. deep. The player, who is usually strolling, hangs it from a leather strap around his shoulders so that both hands are free to strike the drum. The right hand strikes the lower surface with a thin stick producing the light beat, while the left hand, using a thicker, cane-shaped stick, produces the heavier beat. Although the dahal is made in various sizes and thicknesses, the shallow variety is most common. Like the tombak, the skin of the dahal is fixed and cannot be loosened or tightened.

The dayereh is a tambourine larger than the Western variety, often measuring more than 50 cm. in diameter. Instead of circular metal clappers along the rim, the dayereh has a great number of very small metal rings fixed to the inner rim that jingle when struck. (The daff does not have these rings.) This tambourine is an extremely popular instrument in Islamic countries. Before the tombak became prevalent, they were the most widely used percussion instruments, and whenever musicians were depicted in miniatures, they were included. Today they are still used as folk instruments, especially to accompany dancing.

The name naghareh indicates a large class of kettledrums that come in pairs, one larger than the other. They range from a

---

46. Sachs, *History of Musical Instruments*, p. 248.

size resembling the bongo drums used in popular Western music to a size so large that they are carried by donkeys and even camels. The body of the naghareh is made either of copper or heavy pottery, to which the sheepskin or cowskin is attached by means of ropes. In contrast to the tombak and dahal, the naghareh can be tuned by tightening or loosening the strings. The naghareh are struck with wooden sticks.

These kettledrums gave their name to that special kind of music formerly found throughout Persia, the Persian tower music called *Naghareh Khaneh*. In nearly every Persian city, open towers are found where the musicians gathered to play at sunset, midnight, and dawn. Besides percussion instruments of the nagareh family, even larger kettledrums known as gurgeh[47] were used for this music. The woodwind instruments were the surna (oboe) and the karna. The latter is an extremely long trumpet, often seven or eight feet in length, with a wide bell. Since it has no holes or valves, it is not fundamentally different from the ancient trumpet discovered at Persepolis.

INSTRUMENTS OF HISTORICAL INTEREST

The ʿUd

The single most important instrument of the Middle Eastern peoples is, of course, the ʿud, or lute. At the height of the brilliant Islamic civilization, the lute was to Persian and Arab musicians what the piano has been to Europeans since the nineteenth century—the chief instrument not only for musical practice, but for theory as well. The works of al-Farabi, Ibn Sina, and Safi al-Din discuss in great detail the different systems of fretting the lute and the intervals that could be obtained on the instrument.[48]

Although the lute retains its importance in the Arab countries today and is still the most popular non–Western instrument, it has virtually disappeared from Iran.[49] Its present existence in

47. Khaleqi, *SMI*, p. 209.
48. Al-Farabi, *MA*, I, 164–193; Ibn Sina, *MA*, II, 234–243; Safi al-Din, *MA*, III, 371–375, 430–443. Summaries of these discussions of the fretting of the lute may be found among Farmer's writings, in Rouanet's articles in *LavE*, and in Owen Wright's article.
49. Baghdad, one of the centers of Arabic music, hence an important center of lute playing, is less than one hundred miles from the western border of Iran.

A girl at the Conservatory of National Music playing the ʿud.

Persia is due almost entirely to the efforts of the Ministry of Culture, which is trying to revive this instrument. To this end, the ʿud is used in the orchestras of native instruments sponsored by the Ministry, and it is also taught to a few students in the Conservatory of National Music. It is not, to my knowledge, played outside of these circles, and there are no longer virtuoso ʿud players in Tehran. The ʿud played in Iran is like the instrument used in the Arab countries except that the Persians, with their usual flair for elegance, use an eagle's feather as a plectrum instead of the bone or plastic used by the Arabs.

As early as the Sassanian period, the Persians had an ʿud called the barbat. This was the instrument played by the famous musician Barbad and that represented in Sassanian art.[50] The construction was different from that of the Arab lute, since in the barbat, the body and neck were constructed of one graduated piece of

---

50. Pope and Ackerman, *Survey of Persian Art*, plate 208-a.

A student at the Conservatory of National Music playing the qanun.

wood, in contrast to the Arab ʿud, where the two were separate.[51] According to Farmer, this Persian lute was taken to Arabia in A.D. 684 by Persian slaves brought to work at Mecca, the new capital of Islam. It remained in favor in Arabia until the second half of the eighth century, when Zalzal invented a new lute, subsequently used by both Arabs and Persians.[52] It was this new instrument that was brought to Europe through the Arab invasions of Spain, where it reached the height of its development as a Western instrument in the sixteenth century.[53]

In Persia, the lute was the chief instrument for art music until the Safavid period. Frequently represented in miniatures, it is also found among the wall paintings at Chehel Sotun. The long-necked tambur, second to the ʿud in popularity during the Islamic period, seems to have gradually gained in importance until, during the eighteenth century, it superseded the lute. The origins of the tar and its relation to the lute are interesting

51. Farmer, "Ud," in *Encyclopedia of Islam.*
52. Farmer, *History of Arabian Music,* p. 73.
53. The name *lute* is derived from the Arabic *al ʿud.*

problems that may be solved when more treatises and manuscripts of the seventeenth and eighteenth centuries are discovered.

The Qanun

Like the ʿud, the qanun, a plucked zither, is still of great importance for classical music in Arab countries, but has virtually
disappeared from Persia. It, too, is now being revived by the
Persian Ministry of Culture, that is, used in orchestras of native
music and taught in the Conservatory of National Music. The
qanun is slightly larger than the santur, and three of its sides
are perpendicular. The strings are usually of gut or nylon, not
wire. The chief difference between the two instruments is that the
qanun is plucked rather than struck. A player uses small bone
quills attached to his fingers by means of metal rings. One
advantage the qanun has compared to the santur is its tuning.
Whereas on the santur the pitch of each string is fixed for the
length of a single composition, on the qanun the pitch can easily
be raised or lowered by means of levers while playing.

The Ghaychek

A third instrument presently subject to the attentions of the
Ministry of Culture is the ghaychek, a bowed strong instrument
of most unusual shape. The ghaychek, said to have a pre-Islamic
origin in Iran,[54] is still played as a folk instrument in the eastern
provinces of Iran and also in Afghanistan and Pakistan. A
ghaychek has a rounded back and a flat face. The face is elliptical
in overall shape, with a half-circle cut out of either side. Its
neck is short and jointed. The lower half of the face is covered
with skin, with the bridge supporting the strings attached
to the membrane. The instrument usually has a great number of
strings, but of these only two are used for playing, the rest for
resonance. The sound of the ghaychek is rasping and exotic.

"City ghaychek-ha," those presently reconstructed in Tehran,

54. Khaleqi, *SMI*, p. 59.

A folk musician from Baluchistan playing a ghaychek.

are made in three sizes corresponding to the violin, viola, and cello. They have four strings and are tuned like their counterparts in the violin family. These instruments, used in the Ministry of Culture's orchestras, are played by professional violinists.

The Chang

The musical instrument most often depicted in Persian art, both ancient and medieval, and also the one most celebrated in Persian literature is the chang. This harp is clearly represented in the Elamite relief of Malamir, dating from the seventh century B.C., which portrays three musicians: one is playing a triangular harp, and one a cithara or lyre; the third instrument, unfortunately, has deteriorated beyond recognition.[55] Several boatloads of harpists are found accompanying the boar hunters in the Sassanian rock carvings at Taq-i Bustan. During the Islamic period, the chang became famous in literature. Two well known Persian poets were also noted harpists: Rudaki, who lived during the rule of the Samanids at the end of the ninth century and beginning of the tenth,[56] and Farukhi of the eleventh century.[57]

The harp depicted in Persian miniatures of the sixteenth and seventeenth centuries was a large triangular instrument whose body must have been over a meter in length.[58] According to artists' representations, the player supported the lower frame on his knee, and the body, curved at the upper end to form a scroll, was often elaborately decorated. The number of strings varied according to the artists, but usually approached thirty.

Today in Iran, the chang is extinct as a musical instrument. But it does continue its importance as a motive in the visual arts and is still found in contemporary paintings, metal work, and printed cloth.

55. Farmer suggests that the third instrument may have been a tambourine. "Outline History," p. 2789.

56. Edward G. Browne, *A Literary History of Persia*, 6 vols. (Cambridge, 1928), I, 15–17.

57. Browne, *Literary History of Persia*, II, 124.

58. Pope and Ackerman, *Survey of Persian Art*, plates 861-a, 889, 907, and 974-a.

CONCLUSION

At the beginning of this chapter I mentioned the debt Europe owes to the Middle East for the predecessors of most of her musical instruments. In acknowledging this debt, I must now remark that Europe has repaid it in full. History has once more completed a cycle; whereas the Middle East sent to Europe a large number of instruments during the ancient and medevial periods, Europe is now returning these instruments in a technically refined form. The flow of instruments from East to West has been reversed. Today the direction is from West to East, and European instruments are found throughout the Middle East and much of Asia. Not only are they used for European music, but they often replace indigenous instruments for native art music. In Iran, as has been seen, the violin is now one of the principal instruments of Persian music. Furthermore, music of the radif is "unblushingly rendered on the piano and clarinet."[59]

Nonetheless, a small number of traditional Persian instruments appear to have a sort of permanence. Perhaps a certain timbre or special cultural and historical connotations have preserved their places. Or it may be that there is not an exact counterpart among European instruments. At this writing, the tar, sehtar, santur, and tombak do not seem to be in immediate danger of replacement by European instruments. It must be pointed out, however, that their survival depends mainly upon the continued existence of the traditional music played on them. The problem of the endurance of Persian art music is one of great cultural complexity. Europe's music travels even faster than do her musical instruments, reaching a wider audience through the mass media than one composed only of the musicians who play the instruments. Problems of preserving this music and the attempts to solve them, form a conclusion to the present work.

59. Henry G. Farmer, "Persian Music," in *Groves Dictionary of Music and Musicians* 5th ed., ed Eric Blom (1954).

7   Traditional Persian Music in Modern Iran

Rapid transformations in modern Iranian life are severely threatening traditional Persian music. During the last half century, a growing preference for Western culture has not only displaced much traditional Persian art, but has also produced a kind of hybrid art of Persian and Western parentage. The predilection of Iranians for Western sounds is readily observable. Not only is Western classical and popular music widely played in all the cities of Iran, but also much of the native Persian music performed today has been harmonized, orchestrated, and altered in subtle ways to resemble foreign music.[1] The interaction between Persian and Western music did not happen suddenly. Western music came to Iran over a century ago, and for the last fifty years, its influence has been especially strong. The development of the present musical situation may be appreciated by reviewing this last century, observing the musicians and institutions it produced.

RECENT HISTORY[2]

One of Persia's greatest modernizing rulers was Nasir ed din Shah Qajar (r. 1848–1896), the first Iranian monarch to visit Europe

---

1. The process of hybridization is viewed with concern by both Iranian and foreign musicologists. In 1961 UNESCO sponsored a conference in Tehran for the purpose of examining the trend of hybridization and taking measures to control it. The notes of the conference have been published as William Kay Archer, ed., *The Preservation of Traditional Forms of the Learned Music of the Orient and the Occident* (Urbana, Illinois, 1964).

2. Most of the information on recent musical history in Iran is found in the second volume of Khaleqi's *SMI* and in the third volume, *Musik-e Iran*, nos. 89–97 (1959–1960).

since Xerxes and the ruler who began the westernization of Iranian institutions. One of Nasir ed din Shah's innovations was to obtain foreign experts, among them a *chef de musique*, Bousquet, who, with his assistant Rouillon, came to Iran in 1856 on loan from the French government. Bousquet remained in Iran only two years, but Rouillon stayed until 1867. In 1868 a third Frenchman arrived, Alfred Jean Baptiste Lemaire (b. 1842), who stayed in Iran for over forty years and, in fact, died there. He put together what must have been a rather good military band with instruments brought from France.[3] Of more permanent value was his establishing a school of music to train military musicians and music administrators. This later expanded into a nonmilitary school of music which exists today as the major conservatory of music in Iran.

After Lemaire's death in 1909, Gholem Reza Minbashian, grandfather of the present Minister of Culture and a student of Lemaire, became director of the school. With only a few exceptions, the directors of the Conservatory have continued to be Persians. This school was greatly improved, and Persian music was introduced into the curriculum under the directorship of one of the most important figures in modern Iranian music, Colonel Ali Naqi Vaziri (b. 1887).

The son of a general in the Imperial Iranian Army, Vaziri attended military school in Tehran and served as an officer in the army. At the same time he studied music on his own and under a number of masters in Tehran. In 1918, at the age of thirty-one he left for Paris to continue his musical education, studying piano, harmony, and voice at the École Supérieure de Musique. After three years, Vaziri moved to Berlin, where, with the idea of starting his own conservatory in Iran along European lines, he observed all the classes as the Hochschule für Musik and studied counterpoint and composition. In 1923 Vaziri returned to Iran

---

3. The beginning of Lemaire's career in Iran is described by Victor Advielle in *La musique chez les persans* (Paris, 1885). This book also contains (p. 10) a program of dinner music by Lemaire's students at Tehran in 1882—a program that featured music by Gounod, Verdi, Bellini, Donizetti, and Halévy!

One of the earliest public concerts.

and founded his conservatory, the Madresse-ye Ali-ye Musiqi.[4] This school lasted until 1935, when Vaziri left it to become professor of aesthetics at Tehran University.

In the following years, Vaziri's contributions to the development of Persian music were manifold. He wrote several books on the theory of Persian music and published the first collection of Persian music transcribed in Western staff notation.[5] In addition, Vaziri composed a considerable quantity of Persian music in the European idiom, performing it along with more traditional Persian music and Western music at several yearly concerts given by conservatory students. Twice the director of

4. Colonel Vaziri's return from Europe was not the only momentous event of 1923. In that year another colonel, Reza Khan, became Prime Minister of Iran, and the last Qajar Monarch left for Europe, never to return. Two years later, Colonel Reza Khan was crowned Shah of Iran, beginning the present Pahlavi dynasty. His progressive, rather antireligious rule, gave music its chance, and musical activities were practiced much more openly than they had been for many centuries. Thus, the two colonels in quite different ways helped bring about the modernization of Iranian music.

5. Vaziri's publications include *Dastur-e Tar* (Berlin, 1913; Tehran, 1936); *Dastur-e Violin* (Tehran, 1933); *Musiqi-e Nazari* (Tehran, 1934); and numerous collections of folk songs, tasnifs, and suites. Khaleqi's volume of *SMI*, II, is a biography of Vaziri.

Ali Naqi Vaziri leading a group of his students in a concert.

the government's Conservatory of Music (from 1927 to 1934 and from 1941 to 1946), Vaziri also administered the music section of Radio Iran. Although Henry Farmer described Vaziri as the "aged Professor of Aesthetics" in the 1954 edition of Grove's Dictionary,[6] in 1965 Vaziri appeared not at all aged, but most vigorous and enthusiastic, still eager to argue vociferously the merits of quarter tones in Iranian music. Ali Naqi Vaziri is responsible for injecting new life into music in Iran and specifically into native Persian music. Although he had spent several years studying in Europe, Vaziri's intention was not to teach Western music per se, but to use it for the revitalization of Iranian music.

Vaziri's successor in these many efforts was Ruhollah Khaleqi, (1906–1965). Khaleqi studied in Vaziri's conservatory when it was first opened and became a teacher of theory and harmony at the

6. S.v. "Vaziri."

Ruhollah Khaleqi and Ali Naqi Vaziri (holding the sehtar) in the summer of 1965.

government school of music during Vaziri's directorship. After graduating from Tehran University in 1934 with a degree in literature, he entered the Ministry of Education, alternating his work between there and teaching in the School of Music. In 1945 Khaleqi founded the Society for National Music, the aim of which was to encourage native Persian music. The orchestra of this society presented concerts of only Persian music—tasnif-ha, folk songs, and compositions by Vaziri. This group was the predecessor of an extremely significant institution, the Conservatory of National Music, also founded by Khaleqi. Unlike Vaziri's private conservatory which had closed its doors in 1935 and the government school of music, the Conservatory of National Music taught only Persian music. It is now a complete secondary school with over one hundred students and has a postgraduate class in musicology. Emphasis is placed upon the teaching of traditional Persian music and musical instruments; but it is significant that in recent years, more and more Western music and westernized Persian music is entering the curriculum. Affiliated with this conservatory are two night schools where instruction is given without charge in order to encourage amateur musicians to play Persian music.

From 1940 until his death in 1965, Khaleqi worked in the music department of Radio Iran arranging Iranian music for orchestra and writing programs about Iranian music and musicians. He was also Iran's most prolific writer on music, producing six books and numerous magazine articles.[7]

Vaziri and Khaleqi may be considered leaders of the progressive branch of twentieth-century Persian music. With their strong Western orientation balanced by an equally strong sense of the value of traditional Persian culture, they changed the entire course of music and music education in Iran. A more conservative and less active group of musicians who contributed to the preserving rather than the modernizing of Persian music are the followers of Mirza Abdullah, the master credited with the present version of the radif. At his death in 1917, Mirza Abdullah had had a large number of students to whom he had taught his radif. Several were inspired enough to undertake the formidable task of transcribing it. The two most successful were Mehdi Gholi Hedayat, who shares with Vaziri credit for the earliest Iranian attempts to use Western notation for Persian music,[8] and Mussa Maʿruffi.[9]

---

7. Khaleqi's publications include *Nazari be Musiqi*, 2 vols. (Tehran, 1937–1938); *Sargozasht-e Musiqi-e Iran*, 2 vols. (Tehran, 1954–1955); *Ham Ahang-e Musiqi* (Tehran, 1941); and *Musiqi-ye Iran* (Tehran, 1963). His musical compositions include also collections of notated pieces for use in the Conservatory of National Music and collections of harmonized tasnif-ha and instrumental pieces.

8. Alfred Lemaire was probably the first to make extensive transcriptions of Iranian music in Western notation. Several of these are in *LavE*, pp. 3077–3083. A much earlier transcription is found in the *Dictionnaire de la musique* by Jean Jacques Rousseau (Paris, 1768), plate N.

9. *MTI*.

Mirza Abdullah (d. 1917), who classified the present radif.

The most influential teacher of Persian music during this period was Abol Hassan Saba (d. 1957).[10] For many years he conducted private music lessons in his home and later taught in the Conservatory of National Music. While most of the present generation of performers were trained by Saba, their students study the radif from his printed instruction manuals. Also influential for the development of contemporary Persian music was Darvish Khan (d. 1926), inventor of the pish-daramad. As a performer, Darvish Khan participated in one of the landmarks of Persian music—the first European phonograph recordings. During the years between the granting of the Persian constitution (1906) and World War I, Darvish Khan and a number of other musicians made three trips to Europe to record Persian classical music for His Master's Voice.

For the past three decades, the state has taken a large part in Iran's artistic development. This began under the rule of Reza Shah Pahlavi (r. 1925–1941), when there was "what might be termed a cultural revival" as the monarch sought to revitalize native arts and crafts.[11] The government founded the Fine Arts Society in the 1930s, later adding music and ballet sections. In 1950 a new division was established in the Ministry of Education, the State Fine Arts Department, which grew into an enormous organization controlling most of the production and teaching of music, dance, theatre, film, and all visual arts and crafts. In 1964 the Fine Arts Department became a full-scale government ministry under the leadership of Mehrdad Pahlbod, brother-in-law of the present Shah and grandson of Gholem Reza Minbashian, the first Persian director of the Conservatory of Music.

The Ministry of Culture is involved directly or indirectly (mostly directly) with all art music and professional folk music in Persia excepting the music broadcast on the radio, presently a function of the Ministry of Information. The extent of the activities of the Ministry of Culture is vast. For example, in music—merely one of its branches—it administers both the

---

10. A commemorative issue of *Majaleh-ye Musiqi*, vol. 18 (1957), is devoted to the life and works of Saba.

11. Richard Frye, *Iran* (New York, 1953), p. 79.

conservatory where Western music is taught, *Honarestan-e Ali-ye Musiqi*, and the Conservatory of National Music, *Honarestan-e Musiqi-ye Melli*, and it also runs a ballet school. All of these are secondary schools where the pupils study academic subjects in addition to music. It sponsors over a dozen orchestras, including the Tehran Symphony Orchestra, and a professional ballet company. It publishes a monthly music magazine and other major publications of music and sponsors all research into Persian folk and classical music. Finally, the music department of the Ministry of Culture gives nightly television programs, sends musicians abroad for study and for performing, and provides music for functions of the Royal Court.

During the twentieth century, with the more lenient social conditions and the increasing state support described above, there has been a growth of all musical activities in Persia. The patronage of the state is a continuation of court patronage in a sense, but the music it supports is no longer limited to the nobility. Through the mass media, the music sponsored by the Persian government reaches almost all levels of the population, both urban and rural. Thus, music is finally gaining a broader acceptance in Iran and perhaps will soon regain the respectability and eminence accorded it before the Arab conquest.[12]

THE STATE OF CONTEMPORARY PERSIAN MUSIC

A complex and crucial trend in Iran today is the westernization of traditional Persian music. This occurs in two degrees: gross alterations that produce a new hybrid music; and fine modifications in which the texture and character of the Persian music are not radically changed. The drastic changes occur in compositions outside of the radif, that is, in the tasnif, pish-daramad, and reng, the subtler alterations, in the traditional art music within the radif. This is an important distinction: the most traditional music is, by and large, not being used to create new hybrid forms. Rather, the process of hybridization occurs in music that

---

12. See Ella Zonis, "Classical Persian Music in the 1960's," in *Iran Faces the Seventies*, ed. Ehsan Yar-Shater (New York, 1971).

Western instruments being played in ensembles of Persian instruments early in the twentieth century.

is already one step removed from traditional Persian art music, in the nonimprovised compositions that existed side by side with the music of the radif and became more extensively practiced during the first half of the twentieth century.

The first step in westernizing an Iranian tasnif consists in notating the piece and having it played by an orchestra of predominantly Western instruments. In these tasnif-ha, the orchestra doubles the singer in unison and in octaves and adds short ritornelli between sections of the song. A further modification is harmonization of the melody. For many years Vaziri, Khaleqi, and others have investigated the possibilities of harmonizing the Persian scales in such a way that their basic character would be preserved. Such harmonization presents several difficulties given the special peculiarities of Persian music—for example, the use of microtones, the frequent absence of a clear tonic and dominant, and the distinctly modal character of many melodies. The solutions reached by these Persian composers are still hotly debated in musicological circles, although, in practice, they are widely used. The tasnif-ha now played on radio and on television have rudimentary four-part harmony and simple counterpoint (see Example 107).

Larger compositions that have been arranged from these orchestrated tasnif-ha are symphonic suites. Most often, composers of suites merely join two or three tasnif-ha or orchestrated folk songs, but sometimes the transitional material between songs is extended, making the form somewhat more elaborate.

An orchestra of the Ministry of Art and Culture in 1964, containing both
Western and Persian instruments.

While attempts to adapt Persian music to the Western idiom
predominate, a few Persian musicians are working from a
different direction, that is, composing Western music using
Persian melodies as thematic material. Compared to the music
just discussed, these compositions based on Persian themes
generally have thinner texture and are in a more contrapuntal
idiom. Although they are less Persian than the orchestrated
tasnif-ha, they tend to be much more sophisticated and, on the
whole, more successful as music. Most of these compositions are
written abroad by expatriate Persian composers. One of the few
residents of Iran who writes in this idiom is Malek Aslanian, an
Iranian of Armenian background who received his musical
education in Hamburg. In the passage from one of his compositions

given in Example 112, the subject, measures 1–4, is from the naghmeh of Dashti.

EXAMPLE 112.   The opening of a composition in Dashti, by Emanual Malek Aslanian

The second degree in the process of westernization of Persian music, that is, fine changes that do not distort the basic texture and character of the music, occurs in the solo literature of the music of the radif. We have previously noted the increasing use of rhythmic pieces in contrast to the more traditional unmeasured style or avaz. Looking at the radif of Saba, which is reputedly, "more modern" than that of Maʿruffi, we found a greater number of compositions of the zarbi or rhythmic type. There are also changes in the harmonic idiom. Recently some of the microtones have been changed to full half tones. For example, an

F-sori is now often changed to an F-sharp. Then there is the growing popularity for arpeggios on the tonic triad. Although this added flourish at the conclusion of a gusheh is widely played, it is not part of the traditional radif and is not included in any printed versions.[13] Finally, it is becoming more and more usual to color passages by the addition of simultaneous thirds to one or more notes.

These changes in the radif are not radical, nor are they occurring rapidly. In themselves, they do not constitute a threat to the continuation of traditional Persian music. A far more serious development is that the radif is now studied and performed less and less. At the Conservatory of National Music, students do study the radif and may spend several years in the process. But as they become more advanced, they prefer to play instrumental tasnif-ha and other rhythmic pieces that are admittedly more attractive to young people conditioned by Western music from the radio and cinemas of Tehran.

It is, of course, an oversimplification to credit these changes solely to the effects of westernization. A broader trend in Iranian life is the popularization of culture. As we have noted, classical music was once reserved for an elite audience; it is now widely broadcast over the mass media. This in itself causes changes such as the above-mentioned style shift from the unmeasured avaz style to measured pieces that are lighter. That these changes occur in the direction of popular Western styles is no mere coincidence. Yet it might be more correct to discuss them under the rubric of modernization, rather than westernization.

AN EVALUATION

In a country such as Iran, where musical values are in an obvious state of transition, the intervention of the government to concentrate and direct the sensitive cultural process of adapting traditional music to modern tastes is a mixed blessing. The patronage of such a powerful organization is of course to the overall advantage of music. With governmental support and encouragement,

13. A cadence formula that is typically Persian is the *bal-e kabutar*. See p. 93.

An orchestra of the Ministry of Art and Culture dressed in eighteenth-century costumes. The instruments shown are: front row, qanun and ʿud; second row, five ghaychek and a kamanchay; third row, tombak, nay, two tar, two large ghaychek, and two kamanchay.

music has become acceptable, and the long quiescence of traditional Persian music is almost ended. However, the sheer weight of bureaucracy often functions to crush the creative process. Inevitably, the artistic level is lowered when the artist is burdened with myriad rules and administrative details. This is the present situation in Iran.

In Tehran today it is virtually impossible for a Persian musician to make his living by music without being affiliated with the Ministry of Art and Culture or the Ministry of Information.[14] But a frequent complaint of Persian musicians is that becoming an employee of the government restricts one's freedom immeasurably. Musicians must write and play the kind of westernized Persian music or traditional Persian music favored by the current administration. Indeed, the control of the bureaucracy

14. It is often difficult to live even when one *is* employed by a ministry, and most musicians hold two jobs, one usually being nonmusical. This practice is not recent, however; since music was frowned upon for so long, it was usual for Persian musicians to make careers in other professions.

A Tehran music shop window containing traditional Persian instruments and Western guitars, showing that the owner gives no thought to the problems of preservation and westernization.

appears to be so considerable and the personal disagreement so intense that some Persian musicians and musicologists prefer to live abroad. There is virtually no room for musical dissent in Iran.

An unfortunate result of this strong governmental control is that it has produced a standardization in Iranian music—a standardization at a rather mediocre level. Although a great amount of time and effort is being invested in writing orchestrated tasnif-ha, the results are still disappointing. The music produced, with few exceptions, is neither good Persian music nor good Western music. The sensitivity and profundity of the original Persian melody have been destroyed by the thick orchestration and the endless repetition of simple chord progressions.

Even though a solution to the problem of traditional Persian music in modern Iran has not yet been found and so many of the attempts at solution are disappointing, there are positive aspects to the present condition. First, let us be aware of the obvious fact that traditional Persian music still exists, and very many people are concerned with the continuation of its existence. There is a conscious musicological concern for collecting traditional Iranian music, transcribing it, and publishing it. Although the radif published by the Iranian government is not musicologically perfect,[15] it is significant that it was done at all, that it was done so well, and that it was done in Iran. Furthermore, a growing number of historical, analytical, and acoustical studies of Persian music are being made—and by Iranians.[16]

The concern for traditional Persian music is not limited to a scholarly pursuit; prodigious efforts are being made to keep the music alive and to revitalize it. The Minister of Culture is musically knowledgeable and sincerely interested in the problems of modernizing Iranian music to make it attractive to young people.

Thus, on the whole, the future of Persian music seems promising. Taking into account the history of music in Persia—the most distinguishing feature of which is its lack of practice due to centuries of religious disapprobation—it is clear that music was never so widely performed and so well thought of as it is now.

---

15. It was reviewed by this author in *Ethnomusicology* 8 (September 1964), pp. 303–310.

16. An institution with great importance for the preservation of classical Persian music is the recently founded music department at the University of Tehran.

This is a period of abundant musical activity, probably a more musical time than any before it. Even though all this activity is not devoted solely to Persian music, and the greater musical talents are often attracted to Western music, Persian music is by no means neglected and is receiving a large share of the total musical consideration and financial support. In fact, the amount of Persian music played and the percentage of the population it reaches is undoubtedly greater than ever before.

It is too early to judge the efforts to preserve and to modernize Persian music. We must wait until the musical techniques of harmony and counterpoint are assimilated so that they no longer dominate the composition and overwhelm the delicate Persian melodies. The problem of changing Persian music without destroying it will be solved with greater success when Iran develops a national school of composers equally familiar with Persian and Western music or produces a composer of genius who is able to fuse the two styles in a way yet untried.

Appendixes   Bibliography   Discography   Index

Appendix A The Medieval Rhythmic Modes

The best summary and analysis of the medieval rhythmic modes now available is hidden in a monograph that deals with certain Hebrew-script manuscripts of the Jewish philosopher Saʿadyah Gaon.[1] Here, Henry Farmer discusses the problem of interpreting the Islamic rhythmic modes as they are given by theorists from the time of al-Kindi (ninth century) to Safi al-Din (thirteenth century). Needless to say, interpretation is not simply a matter of transcribing the theorists' descriptions of the modes into modern notation, for medieval Arabic terminology tends to be extremely vague. Furthermore, there is often complete disagreement among theorists regarding any one particular rhythm. Working with numerous sources, Farmer has reached one solution to the problem of the rhythmic modes, which is the basis for the following discussion.

THE NOTATION OF RHYTHM

Medieval Persian and Arab musicians notated rhythm by means of an onomatopoetic system based on syllables used for prosody.[2] A second syllabic notation, used only for music and not for poetry, employed the syllable "ta" and contained combinations such as "ta + tan, ta + ta + tan." There was also a third rhythmic tablature that employed dots. In this method, each dot denoted a beat; the open dot "o" was a struck beat, and the closed dot "·" was either a rest or a continuation of the struck beat. Thus, "o·" could be either a quarter note followed by a quarter rest or two

---

1. *Saʿadyah Gaon on the Influence of Music* (London, 1943).
2. See above, pp. 58–61.

quarters notes tied. A fourth scheme used by the theorists took the form of circular diagrams. The rhythmic mode ramal (in chapter 5) as given by the medieval theorist Safi al-Din is notated below in all four systems.[3]

1. muf-ta^c-i-la-tun fa-^ci-lun

2. tan ta ta tan tan ta ta tan

3. o· o o   o· o·   o o o·

4.

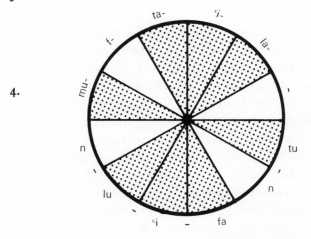

(Each segment is a beat and the shaded segments are struck.)

THE RHYTHMIC FEET

The Islamic poetic feet, units corresponding to the iamb, trochee, spondee, and so forth, were first listed by al-Farabi, who divided them into two classes, conjunct feet, in which the time values are equal, and disjunct feet, in which they are not. According to Farmer's interpretation, these feet are as follows:[4]

CONJUNCT

Sari (quick)   ♪

Khafif (light)   ♪ ⁊   or   ♩

3. D'Erlanger, MA, III, 171.
4. Farmer, Sa^cadyah Gaon, pp. 74–76.

Khafif al thaqil (light heavy) ♪ 𝄾 𝄾   𝅗𝅥.

Thaqil (heavy) ♪ 𝄾 𝄾 𝄾   𝅗𝅥

DISJUNCT: first group

Sari ♫ 𝄾   ♪ 𝅗𝅥

Khafif ♪ 𝄾 ♪ 𝄾 𝄾   𝅗𝅥 𝅗𝅥.

Khafif al thaqil ♪ 𝄾 𝄾 ♪ 𝄾 𝄽   𝅗𝅥. 𝅗𝅥

Thaqil ♪ 𝄾 𝄽 ♪ 𝄾 𝄾 𝄽   𝅗𝅥 𝅗𝅥♪

DISJUNCT: second group, equal

Sari ♫♪ 𝄾   ♫ 𝅗𝅥

Khafif ♪ 𝄾 ♪ 𝄾 ♪ 𝄾 𝄾   𝅗𝅥 𝅗𝅥 𝅗𝅥.

Khafif al thaqil ♪ 𝄾 𝄾 ♪ 𝄾 𝄾 ♪ 𝄾 𝄽   𝅗𝅥. 𝅗𝅥. 𝅗𝅥

Thaqil ♪ 𝄾 𝄽 ♪ 𝄾 𝄽 ♪ 𝄾 𝄽 𝄾   𝅗𝅥 𝅗𝅥 𝅗𝅥 𝅗𝅥♪

DISJUNCT: second group, unequal

Hathith ♫ 𝄾 ♪ 𝄾 𝄾   ♪ 𝅗𝅥 𝅗𝅥

Khafif ♪ 𝄾 ♪ 𝄽 ♪ 𝄾 𝄽   𝅗𝅥 𝅗𝅥. 𝅗𝅥

Khafif al thaqil ♪ 𝄾 𝄾 ♪ 𝄾 𝄽 ♪ 𝄾 𝄾 𝄽   𝅗𝅥. 𝅗𝅥 𝅗𝅥♪

   Most medieval writers list eight modes constructed of these
feet; but although there is fairly good agreement on the names
of the modes, there is little consensus among the theorists on the
actual rhythms represented by the names. The eight most
common modes, or iqaᶜat, according to al-Kindi (d. ca. 874) and
Saᶜadyah Gaon (d. 942), are listed below. (This version is not
valid for the following centuries since the versions of these same
modes given by later theorists are often in disagreement.)

1. Al thaqil al awwal $\frac{4}{2}$ 𝅗𝅥 𝅗𝅥 𝅗𝅥 –

2. Al thaqil al thani $\frac{4}{2}$ 𝅗𝅥 𝅗𝅥 – 𝅗𝅥

3. Al Makhuri $\frac{5}{8}$ ♪ 𝅗𝅥 ♪ 𝄾

4. Khafif al thaqil $\frac{4}{8}$ ♩ ♫ ♪   𝄿

5. Al Ramal $\frac{4}{4}$ ♩ 𝄾 ♩ ♩

6. Khafif al ramal $\frac{3}{8}$ ♫ ♪

7. Khafif al khafif $\frac{3}{8}$ ♪ ♪   𝄿

8. Al Hazaj $\frac{4}{8}$ ♪ ♪   𝄾

Appendix B   Excerpts from the Bahjat al Ruh^c

CHAPTER 7.   THE MUSIC SUITED TO EACH CLASS OF GATHERING

In a gathering of sleek pale-skinned men, the musician should play . . . soft low-pitched modes such as Iraq, Rast, Mukhalaf, Nihuft, and kindred modes, from which listeners of this class, who have a natural freshness of mind, derive great gaiety and gladness, sharing in the pleasure they bring.

In a gathering whose members are dark-skinned, lean and thin, the musician should strike the strings quickly and sharply playing such tunes as Sihgah [sic], Nairiz, Zabul, Maghlub and Salmak and kindred tunes. The hearers get so much satisfaction that they are ready to offer all they possess, regardless of cost, to the master of music.

In a gathering where the members are of moderate size and sallow complexion, the musician should play moderate and steady melodies such as Ushshaq, Rahawi, Hajaz, Gavasht and Ajam.

In a festive gathering where the men are tall and tawny, he should sing Zangula, Nahawandar, Rahawi, Hajaz, Bu Salik and Panjgah. If the audience is not responsive, he should change his melodies and sing the exact opposite. When hearing this, they recall what the musician first played and yield to his choice.

To an audience of men with small heads and big faces, the musician should play the shadd of Dugah and Husaini. If they have large heads and small teeth, he should play Mukhalaf and Iraq. If they are very tall and pale-skinned, the musician should play Mahur and Hajaz, as the movements of the seven planets dictate.

1. See chapter 1, note 49.

Amongst soldiers and their leaders, men of the sword, Turks and fighting men, the musician should play melodies starting in a low pitch and ending in a high one, such as Rast, Panjgah, Iraq, Dugah and Neigiz.

[Other classes included in this description are the following: a gathering of artisans and people of the market; a gathering of kings; when the audience consists of scholars and the like; an audience of needy men; when amongst musicians, poets and intellectuals; a gathering of women; a gathering of men who work with fire.

And the writer concludes by stating that "in short the musician should adapt his music to the planet in the horoscope of his listeners."]

CHAPTER 10.   BEHAVIOR OF THE MUSICIAN

You should know, dear reader, that this humble servant, who has spent much of his time in the honorable company of kings, proud princes and famous ministers of his time, has found certain modes of conduct to be indispensable to the musician if he is not to fall in their estimation.

1.   The less the musician is seen by the outside world the greater will be the respect in which he is held.

2.   He must pay great attention to being well dressed.

3.   He should avoid cold and dry food.

4.   He should daily lift heavy stones and carry them a few steps.

5.   He should be moderate in his intercourse with women.

6.   He should have sufficient physical exercise.

7.   He should not be averse from eating manna, unboiled milk and live oil to keep his voice clear and in good condition.

8.   Every day he should sing and memorize songs, both easy and difficult, teaching them also to novices so that they become part of his technique.

9.   He should not sing a tune which he has not thoroughly memorized.

10.   He should not show over-eagerness to play or sing, as the audience may resent it.

11.   When he performs before kings and society people and in

houses given to pleasure or license, he should then and there forget anything wrong and improper that takes place and not mention it to other audiences as repetition of it may be the cause of harm and ill feelings amongst friends.

12.   He should not indulge in buffoonery and should avoid coarse jokes and expressions and not whisper with the attendants and servants of the master of the assembly nor promote discord amongst them.

13.   He should not cast improper glances towards the women and their attendants.

14.   His musical instruments should not be defective, but always ready to play and not take too long to tune. The perfect instruments are five in number: the lute of the sun; the flute of Mercury; the kamanche of Venus; the surna of Saturn; and the balaban of Mars. All other instruments are defective and do not produce the sounds that are wanted or meant.

15.   The musician should include in his repertory the 3 difficult compositions (tasnif) of Immam Fakhr ud din Ta^cusi Haraqi which contain the 12 principal rhythmic modes, *usul*, 3 rhythmic phrases, *daur*, the 12 principal melodic modes and the 24 branch modes.

[The author then gives these three compositions by writing the words, the melodic mode, and writing out the "tan tana" rhythmic pattern. Next he prescribes music for each season and for in-between seasons.]

There are four *shadd* in music:
1.   Shadd of Nawa and Nishaburak, fiery and eastern.
2.   Shadd of Dugah, Husaini, windy and western.
3.   Shadd of Rast and Panjgah, watery and northern.
4.   Shadd of Mukhalaf and Iraq, earthy and southern.

It is one's duty to know what melodies (*ahang*) are to be sung at various times of the day: at sunrise, Dugah, Husaini and Sihgah; between sunrise and noon, Mubarqa, Chahargah, Panjgah and Nairiz; at noon, Dugah, Nahawandak, Mahur, Gardaniyya, and Uzzal; in the afternoon, Ushshaw, Nawa,

Busalik, Buzurg, Kuchak, and Gardaniyya; at sunset, Hajaz, Salmak, Maya, Basta Nigar and Esfahan; at night, Gardaniyya, Narrizi, Kabir, Rahawi, Humayun and Nihuft; at bed time, Iraq, Ushshaq, and Rast which inspire courage; at midnight, Zabul, Auj, and Busalik; at false dawn, Nauriz i Khara, Nauriz i Arab, Najaz and Mahur; at the break of dawn, Ajam, Iraq, Basta Nigar, Shahnaz, Rahab and Bayat. In this way the listener will carry the banners of song out of the realm of fancy into the realm of truth and under its influence be led to self-contemplation, self-endeavor, and self-converse, and turning for his wants towards the threshold of God who has not wants.

Bibliography

The following list is not limited to works concerning Persian music, but extends beyond the subject of the present book in certain directions. Among the supplementary items are works on medieval Arabian music, articles concerning Islamic music in Central Asia and India, some of the basic studies of the music of countries neighboring Iran, and complete bibliography of the books and articles (on any subject) written by Henry G. Farmer. For those wishing to extend this bibliography, the following works are extremely useful: "Bibliography of Asiatic Musics," *Notes* 5–7 (1947–1950); J. D. Pearson, *Index Islamicus 1906–1955* (Cambridge, England, 1958), and *Index Islamicus Supplement 1956–1960* (Cambridge, England, 1962).

BOOKS AND ARTICLES IN WESTERN LANGUAGES

Abul Fazl. *Ain i Akbari*. Trans. H. Blockman in *Hindu Music from Various Authors*, ed. S. M. Tagore, pp. 211–216.

Ackerman, Phyllis. "The Character of Persian Music." In *A Survey of Persian Art*, ed. Arthur U. Pope and Phyllis Ackerman, III, 2805–2817.

Advielle, Victor. *La musique chez les persanes en 1885*. Paris, 1885.

Allawerdi, Michael. *The Philosophy of Oriental Music*. Damascus, 1949.

Apel, Willi. "Arab Music," "Intervals,˙ calculation of," "Melody types," "Piano" "Persia." In *Harvard Dictionary of Music*, 2nd ed. Cambridge, 1969.

Arberry, A. J., ed. *Persian Poems*. London, 1954.

——, ed. *Tales from the Masnavi*. London, 1961.

——, ed. *More Tales from the Masnavi*. London, 1963.

——, *Sufism*. London, 1950.

Archer, William K., ed. *The Preservation of Traditional Forms of the Learned Music of the Orient and Occident*. Urbana, Ill. 1964.

Arnold, Thomas, and Alfred Guillaume, eds. *The Legacy of Islam*. Oxford, 1931.

Avenary, Hanoch. "Abu'l-Salt's Treatise on Music." *Musica Disciplina* 6 (1952), 27–32.

Bachmann, Werner. *Die Anfänge des Streichinstrumentenspiels*. 2d ed. Leipzig, 1964.

Baines, Anthony. *Musical Instruments Through the Ages*. London, 1961.

Barkechli, Mehdi. *La résonance dans les echelles musicales*. Paris, 1963.

——, "L'évolution de la gamme dans la musique orientale." *Acoustique musicale* 84 (May 1958).

——, "Musiqi-i Ibn Sina." In *Livre du millenaire d'Avicenne*. Tehran, 1956. II, 466–477.

——, "Musique des 'zour-khaneh' et ses rhythmes caracteristiques." *JIFMC* 13 (1962), 73.

——, "La musique iranienne." In *L'histoire de la musique*, ed. Roland Manuel. *Encyclopédie de la Pléiade*, vol. 9. Paris, 1960.

——, *La musique traditionelle de l'Iran*. Tehran, 1963.

——, "Quelques idées nouvelles sur la consonance." *Acoustique musicale* 84 (May 1958).

——, "Les rhythmes caractéristiques de la musique iranienne." In *Bericht über den Siebenten Internationalen Musikwissenschaftlichen Kongress*. Cologne, 1958.

Beichert, E. A. "Die Wissenschaft der Musik bei al-Farabi." *Kirchenmusikalisches Jahrbuch* 27 (1932).

Belaiev, V. "Turkish Music." *Musical Quarterly* 20 (1935), 356–357.

Berner, A. *Studien zum arabischen Musik auf Grund der genenwartigen Theorie und Praxix in Ägypten*. Leipzig, 1937.

Bhanu, D. "Promotion of Music by the Turko-Afghan Rulers of India." *Islamic Culture* 29 (1955), 9–31.

Blom, Eric. "Farmer, Henry George." In *Grove's Dictionary of Music and Musicians*, 5th ed., ed. Eric Blom. London, 1954.

Bonanni, Filippo. *Gabinetto Armonico*. Rome, 1723. Repr. *The Showcase of Musical Instruments*. New York, 1964.

Borrel, E. "Contribution a là bibliographie de la musique turque au XXe siècle." *Revue des études islamiques* 2 (1928), 513–527.

Boubakeur, Si Hamza. "Psalmodie iranique." In *Encyclopédie des musiques sacrées*, ed. Jacques Porte. Paris, 1968. I, 388–403.

Boyce, Mary. *The Manichean Hymn Cycles in Parthian*. Oxford, 1954.

Brun, Corneille le. *Voyages de Corneille le Brun*. Paris, 1701.

Browne, Edward G. "Barbad and Rudagi: The Minstrels of the Houses of Sasan and Saman." *JRAS* (1899), 54–69.

——, *A Literary History of Persia*. 6 vols. Cambridge, England, 1928.

Buchner, Alexandre. *Musical Instruments Through the Ages*. London, 1956.

Caron, Nelly, and Dariouche Safvate. *Iran: Les traditions musicales*. Institut

International d'Études Comparatives de la Musique. Buchet/Chastel, 1966.

———, "La musique shiite en Iran." In *Encyclopédie de musiques sacrées*, ed. Jacques Porte. Paris, 1968. I, 430–440.

Carmi-Cohen, Dalia. "An Investigation into the Tonal Structure of the Maqamat." *JIFMC* 16 (1964), 102–106.

Chagla, Ahmad G. "Muslim Contribution to Indo-Pakistan Music." *Pakistan Misc.* (1952), 163–168.

Chardin, John. *Voyages du Chevalier Chardin*. 3 vols. Amsterdam, 1735.

Chodzko, A. *Théâtre persan*. Paris, 1878.

Chottin, Alexis. "La musique arabe" In *L'histoire de la musique*, ed. Roland Manuel. *Encyclopédie de la Pléiade*, vol. 9. Paris, 1960.

———, "Panégyriques et musiques religieuses populaires dans la religion musulmane." In *Encyclopédie des musiques sacrées*, ed. Jacques Porte. Paris, 1968. I, 409–413.

———, and Hans Hickman "Arabische Musik." In *Die Musik in Geschichte und Gegenwart*, ed. Fredrich Blume. Kassel, 1949.

Christensen, Arthur. *L'Iran sous les Sassanides*. Copenhagen, 1944.

———, "La vie musicale dans la civilisation des Sassanides." *Bulletin de l'Association Française des Amis de l'Orient* 20/21 (1936).

Christensen, Dieter. "Brautlieder der Hakkari-Kurden." *Jahrbuch für musikalische Volks- und Völkerkunde* 1 (1963), 11–47.

Christianswitsch, M. A. *Esquisse historique de la musique arabe aux temps anciens*. Cologne, 1863.

Christie, A. H. "Islamic Minor Arts." *In The Legacy of Islam*, ed. Thomas Arnold and Alfred Guillaume.

Collangettes, M. "Étude sur la musique arabe." *Journal asiatique* 4 (1904), 356–442; 8 (1906), 225–238.

Crossley-Holland, Peter. "Preservation and Renewal of Traditional Music." *JIFMC* 16 (1964), 15–18.

Curzon, George. *Persia and the Persian Question*. London, 1892.

Dagher, J. A. *Repertoire des bibliotheques du proche et du moyen orient*. Paris. 1951.

Daniel, Francesco S. *La musique arabe*. Algiers, 1893.

———, *La musique arabe*. Edited and with notes, memoir, bibliography, and musical examples by Henry G. Farmer. New York and London, 1915.

Danielou, Alain. *Inde du norde: Les traditions musicales*. Institut International d'Études Comparatives de la Musique. Buchet/Chastel, 1966.

Delor, J. "Musique afghane." *Afghanistan* 3 (1956), 24–29.

D'Erlanger, Rudolph. "Au sujet de la musique arabe en Tunisie." *Revue tunisienne* (1917), 91–95.

———, *La musique arabe*. 6 vols. Paris, 1930–1959.

Deutsche Gesellschaft für Musik des Orients, Mitteilungen, nos. 1–3. Hamburg, 1962–1964.

Donington, Robert. "Ornamentation." In *Grove's Dictionary of Music and Musicians*, 5th ed., ed. Eric Blom. London, 1954.

Elsner, Jürgen. "Rubani, zu Prinzipien vorderorientalischer Musikpraxis." *Beiträge zur Musikwissenschaft*, Jahrg. 7, Heft 3. Berlin, 1965.

———, "Zu Prinzipien arabischer Musierpraxis." *Jahrbuch für musikalische Volks- und Völkerkünde* 3 (1967), 90–95.

Emsheimer, E. "Singing Contests in Central Asia." *JIFMC* 8 (1956), 26–29.

———, *Studia Ethnomusicologica Eurasiatica*. Stockholm, 1964.

Engel, Carl. *Catalogue of Instruments in the South Kensington Museum*. London, 1874.

Farhat, Hormoz. "Persian Classical Music." In *Festival of Oriental Music and the Related Arts*. Los Angeles, 1960.

———, Review of recording: *Musical Anthology of the Orient: Iran*, Alain Danielou. *Ethnomusicology* 6 (1962), 239–241.

———, Review of *Der Dastgah* by Khatchi Khatchi. *Ethnomusicology* 8 (1964), 76–77.

———, "The Dastgah Concept in Persian Music." Ph.D. diss., University of California, Los Angeles, 1965. University Microfilms 66:266.

Farmer, Henry G. *Al-Farabi's Arabic-Latin Writings on Music*. London, 1960.

———, "An Anonymous English-Arabic Fragment on Music." *Islamic Culture* 18 (1944), 201–205.

———, *The Arabian Influence on Musical Theory*. London, 1925.

———, "Arabian Musical Instruments on a Thirteenth Century Bowl." *JRAS* (1950), 110–111.

———, "The Arabic Musical Manuscripts in the Bodleian Library." *JRAS* (1925), 639–654.

———, "Byzantine Musical Instruments in the Ninth Century." *JRAS* (1925), 299–304.

———, "The Canon and Eschaquiel of the Arabs." *JRAS* (1926), 239–256.

———, "Clues for the Arabian Influence on European Musical Theory." *JRAS* (1925), 61–80.

———, "The Congress of Arabian Music" (Cairo, 1932). *Transactions of the Glasgow Oriental Society* 6 (1929–1933), 61–67.

———, "An Early Greek Pandore." In *Oriental Studies: Mainly Musical*. London, 1933.

———, "Early References to Music in the Western Sudan." *JRAS* (1939), 569–579.

———, "Abd al Kadir," "Buk," "Duff," "al-Gharid," "Ghina," "Ibn Misjah," "Ishak al Mausili," "Kitara," "Mukharik," "Muristus," "Mushaka," "Musiki," "Mizaf," "Miznar," "Nawba," "Rabab," "Safi al Din," "Sandj," "Tabl," "Tablkhana," "Tunbur," "Ud," "Zalzal," "Ziryab." In *The Encyclopedia of Islam*, ed. M. T. Houtsma, T. W. Arnold, R. Basset, R. Hartmann. Leiden, 1914–1938.

——, "The Evolution of the Tunbur or Pandore." *Transactions of the Glasgow Oriental Society Society* 5 (1923–1928), 26–28.

——, "A Further Arabic-Latin Writing on Music." *JRAS* (1933), 307–322.

——, " 'Ghosts'—An Excursus on Arabic Musical Bibliographies." *Isis* 104 (1946), 123–29.

——, "Greek Theorists of Music in Arabic Translation." *Isis* 13 (1929–1930), 325–333.

——, "Abd al Qadir," "Al Amuli," "Al Farabi," "Al Ghazali," "Al Isfahani," "Al Jurjani," "Al Khalil," "Al Kindi," "Al Razi," "Al Shalahi," " Al Shirazi," "Al Tusi," "Arabian Music," "Babylonian Music," "Buk," "Egyptian Music," "Hydraulic Organ," "Ibn Abd Rabbihi," "Ibn al Khalib," "Ibn al Nadim," "Ibn Sina," "Ibrahim al Mausili," "Ibrahim al Mahdi," "Iraqian and Mesopotamian Music," "Ishac al Mausili," "Pandore," "Persian Music," "Safi al Din," "Sufi and Dervish Music," "Turkestan (Eastern, Instruments of)," "Turkestani Music," "Turkish Crescent," "Ud," "Zalzal." In *Grove's Dictionary of Music and Musicians*, 5th ed., ed. Eric Blom. London, 1954.

——, *Historical Facts for the Arabian Musical Influence.* London, 1930.

——, *A History of Arabian Music to the XIIIth Century.* London, 1929.

——, "The Horn of Alexander the Great." *JRAS* (1926), 500–503.

——, "Ibn Khurdadhbih on Musical Instruments." *JRAS* (1928), 509–518.

——, "The 'Ihsa al Ulum.' " *JRAS* (1933), 906–909.

——, "The Importance of Ethnological Studies." In *Oriental Studies: Mainly Musical.* London, 1953. 47–50.

——, "The Influence of Al-Farabi's ᶜIhsa alᶜulumᵓ (*De Scientis*) on the Writers on Music in Western Europe." *JRAS* (1932), 561–592.

"The Influence of Music: From Arabic Sources." *Proceedings of the Musical Association* 52 (1926), 89–124.

——, "The Instruments of Music on the Taq-i Bustan Bas-Reliefs." *JRAS* (1938), 397–412.

——, "The Jewish Debt to Arab Writers on Music." *Islamic Culture* 15 (1941), 59–63.

——, ed. *La musique arabe* by Francesco Salvador Daniel.

——, "The Lute Scale of Avicenna." *JRAS* (1937), 245–257.

——, "A Maghribi Work on Musical Instruments." *JRAS* (1935), 339–353.

——, "Maimonides on Listening to Music." *JRAS* (1933), 867–884.

——, "Meccan Musical Instruments." *JRAS* (1929), 489–505.

——, *Military Music.* London, 1950.

——, "The Minstrels of the Golden Age of Islam." *Islamic Culture* 17 (1943), 273–281; 18 (1944), 53–61.

——, *The Minstrelsy of the Arabian Nights.* Bearsden, 1945.

——, "Music." In *the Legacy of Islam*, ed. Thomas Arnold and Alfred Guillaume. 356–375.

————, "The Music of the Arabian Nights." *JRAS* (1944), 172–185; (1945), 40–60.

————, "Music: The Priceless Jewel." *JRAS* (1941), 22–30, 127–144.

————, "The Musical Instruments of the Sumerians and Assyrians." In *Oriental Studies: Mainly Musical*. London, 1953.

————, *Musikgeschichte in Bildern: Islam*. Leipzig, 1967.

————, In The New Oxford History of Music, Vol. 1: *Ancient and Oriental Music*, ed. Egon Wellesz. London, 1960. "The Music of Ancient Egypt," "The Music of Ancient Mesopotamia," "The Music of Islam."

————, "A North-African Folk Instrument." *JRAS* (1928), 25–34.

————, "A Note on the Mizmar and Nay." *JRAS* (1929), 119–121.

————, "An Old Moorish Lute Tutor." *JRAS* (1931), 349–366; (1932), 99–109, 379–389, 897–904; (1937), 117–120.

————, "The Old Arabian Melodic Modes." *JRAS* (1965), 99–102.

————, "The Old Persian Musical Modes." *JRAS* (1926), 93–95.

————, *The Organ of the Ancients*. London, 1931.

————, "The Organ of the Muslim Kingdoms." *JRAS* (1926), 495–499.

————, "Oriental Influences on Occidental Military Music." *Islamic Culture* 15 (1941), 235–242.

————, "The Origin of the Arabian Lute and Rebec." *JRAS* (1930), 767–783.

————, "An Outline History of Music and Music Theory." In *A Survey of Persian Art*, ed. Arthur U. Pope and Phyllis Ackerman. London, 1939. III, 2783–2804.

————, "Persische Musik." Trans. Dieter Christianson, In *Die Musik in Geschichte und Gegenwart*, ed. Fredrich Blume. Kassel, 1962.

————, "Reciprocal Influences on Music Between the Far and Middle East." *JRAS* (1934), 327–342.

————, "The Religious Music of Islam." *JRAS* (1952), 60–65.

————, *Saᶜadyah Gaon on the Influence of Music*. London, 1943.

————, "The Science of Music on the Mafatih al-ᶜulum." *Glasgow University Oriental Society Transactions* 17 (1957–58), 1–9.

————, "Some Musical MSS. Identified." *JRAS* (1926), 91–93.

————, *The Song Captions in the Kitab al-Aghani al-Kabir*. Glasgow, 1955.

————, *The Sources of Arabian Music*. Rev. ed. Leiden, 1965.

————, "The Structure of the Arabain and Persian Lute in the Middle Ages." *JRAS* (1939), 41–51.

————, *Studies in Oriental Musical Instruments*. 1st & 2d Series: London, 1931; Glasgow, 1939.

————, "The Study of the Musical Instruments in Primitive Culture." *Glasgow Oriental Society Transactions* 8 (1936–37), 29–37.

————, "Turkish Instruments of Music in the Fifteenth Century." *JRAS* (1940), 195–198.

————, "Turkish Instruments of Music in the Seventeenth Century." *JRAS* (1936), 1–43.

————, "Was the Arabian and Persian Lute Fretted?" *JRAS* (1937), 453–460.

————, "What is Arabian Music?" In *Oriental Studies: Mainly Musical*. London, 1953. 53–58.

————, "William Hunter and His Arabic Interest." In *Oriental Studies: Mainly Musical*. London, 1953. 27–43.

————, "Zenei Kölcsönhátasok Kelet-és Középázsia Kösott(Wechselwirkungen mittel- und ostasiatischer Musik)." *Emlekkömyu Koldály* (1934), 32–42.n

Forugh, M. "A Comparative Study of Persian Passion Plays and Wester Mystery Plays." *Revue iranienne d'anthropologie* (1957), 55–60.

Frye, Richard. *The Heritage of Persia*. London, 1962.

————, *Iran*. New York, 1953.

Fück, J. " 'Arabische' Musikkultur und Islam." *Orientalistische Literaturzeitung* 48 (1953), 20–27.

Furst, Henri. "Musiques Persanes." *Revue musicale* (1926), 228–235.

Gairdner, W. H. T. "The Source and Character of Oriental Music." *The Moslem World* 6 (1916), 347–356.

Gerson-Kiwi, Edith. "The Bourdon of the East—Its Regional and Universal Trends." *JIFMC* 16 (1964), 49–50.

————, *The Persian Doctrine of Dastga-Composition*. Tel Aviv, 1963.

————, "Migrations and Mutations of Oriental Folk Instruments." *JIFMC* 4 (1962), 16–19.

————, "Religious Chant: A Pan-Asiatic Conception of Music." *JIFMC* 13 (1961), 64–67.

Ghirshman, Romain. *Iran*. Baltimore, Md., 1954.

Gladwin, Frances. "An Essay on Persian Music." *New Asiatic Miscellany* (1789), 261–270.

Gobineau, le Comte de. *Trois ans en Asie*. Paris, 1859.

Gosvami, O. *The Story of Indian Music*. Bombay, 1957.

Grigorian, Roubik. *Cinq chansons rustiques iraniennes*. Tehran, 1949.

————, *Recueil de chanson rustiques iraniennes*. Tehran, 1949.

Grunebaum, G. E. von. *Muhammadan Festivals*. London, 1958.

Hacobian, Zavin. "Improvisation et l'ornamentation en orient et en occident." *JIFMC* 16 (1964), 74–76.

Hafni, Mahmud. *Ibn Sina Musiklehre*. Berlin, 1931.

Haidar, Rizvi, S. N. "Music in Muslim India." *Islamic Culture* 15 (1941), 331–340.

Halim, A. "History of the Growth and Development of North-Indian Music During the Sayyid-Lodi Period." *Journal of the Asiatic Society of Pakistan* (1956), 46–64.

————, "Music and Musicians of the Court of Shah Jahan." *Islamic Culture* 19 (1945), 354–360.

Hamburg, Paul. "Early Jewish Writings on the Philosophy of Music." *Mosaic* 6 (1965), 42–50.

Herodotus. *The Histories*. Trans. Aubrey de Sélincourt. Baltimore, Md., 1954.

Hickmann, Hans. "Aegyptische Musik." In *Die Musik in Geschichte und*

Gegenwart, ed. Fredrich Blume. Kassel, 1951.

———, "Aegypten." In *Musik des Altertums. Musikgeschichte in Bildern*, vol. 2. Leipzig, 1962.

Huart, Clement. "Musique persane." *Encyclopédie de la musique*, ed. Albert Lavignac and Lionel de la Laurencie. Paris, 1922.

Husman, Heinrich. *Grundlagen der antiken und orientalischen Musik-Kultur*. Berlin, 1961.

Idelsohn, A. Z. "Die Maqamen der arabischen Musik." *Sammelbande der International Musik Gesellschaft* 15 (1913), 1–63.

Imamuddin, S. M. "Music in Muslim Spain." *Islamic Culture* 33 (1959), 147–150.

Iskandar, Kai Kavus. *Qabus Nama: A Mirror for Princes*. Trans. Reuben Levy. London, 1951.

Kaldun, Ibn. *Maqaddimah*. Trans. Franz Rosenthal. New York, 1958.

Karpeles, Maud. *The Collecting of Folk Music and Other Ethnomusical Material: A Manual for Field Workers*. London, 1958.

Kaumudi. "Mingling of Islamic and Idigenous Traditions in Indian Music." *Indian Historical Quarterly* 26 (1950), 129–137.

Khaleqi, Ruhollah. "An Introduction to Iranian Music." Speech at the British Council. Tehran, Dec. 10, 1963.

Khatchi, Khatchi. *Der Dastgah*. Regensburg, 1962.

———, "Das Intervallibildungsprinzip des persischen Dastgah Shur." *Jahrbuch für musikalische Volks- und Völkerkünde* 3 (1967), 70–84.

Kieswetter, R. G. *Der Musik der Araber nach Originalquellen dargestellt*. Leipzig, 1842.

Knosp, Gaston. "Notes sur la musique persane." *Le guide musicale* (1909). 283–285, 307–310, 327–330, 347–352.

Kosegarten, J. G. *Alii Ispahanensis: Liber Cantilenarum Magnus*. Greifswald, 1840–1843.

Kunst, Jaap. *Ethnomusicology*. 3d ed. The Hague, 1959.

Lach, R. "Die Musik der turktatatischen, finnischugrischen und Kaukasus-völker in ihrer entwicklungsgeschichtlichen und psychologischen Bedeutung für die Entstehung der musikalischen Formen." *Mitteilungen der Anthropologischen Gesellschaft in Wien* 50 (1920), 23–50.

Lachmann, Robert, and Mahmud el-Hefni. ed. and trans. *Jaᶜqub Ibn Ishaq al-Kindi: Risala fi hubr taᶜlif al-alhan*. (*Uber die Komposition der Melodien*). Leipzig, 1931.

Lachmann, Robert. "Die Musik in den tunisischen Stadten." *Archiv für Musikwissenschaft* 5 (1923), 136–171.

———, *Musik des Orients*. Breslau, 1929.

———, "Musikwissenschaftlische Forschungen in Tunisien." *Forschungen und Fortschritte* 6 (1930), 402–403.

Lachmann, Robert, and A. H. Fox Strangways. "Muhammedan Music." In *Grove's Dictionary of Music and Musicians*, 4th ed., ed. H. C. Colles. London, 1940.

Land, Jan Pieter Nicolaas. *Récherches sur l'histoire de la gamme arabe*. Leiden, 1884. [This work contains the section on instruments from al-Farabi's *Kitab al Musiqi al Kabir* in French and in Arabic translation.]

———, *Essais de notation musicale chez les arabes et les persanes*. Leiden, 1885.

Lasalle, Albert de. "La musique des persans." *Chronique musicale* (1873), 81–85.

List, George. "Acculturation and Musical Tradition." *JIFMC* 16 (1964), 18–21.

Macdonald, D. B. "Emotional Religion in Islam as Affected by Music and Singing." *Royal Asiatic Society Journal* (1901–02).

Mahmoud, Parviz. "A Theory of Persian Music and Its Relation to Western Practice." Ph.D. diss., University of Indiana, 1956.

Majd, Fozieh. "The Issue of the Radifs." *Kayhan International* (Jan. 27, 1964), p. 6.

Malm, William P. *Music Cultures of the Pacific, the Near East, and Asia*. Englewood Cliffs, New Jersey, 1967.

Marcuse, Sibyl. *Musical Instruments: A Comprehensive Dictionary*. New York, 1964.

Marlowe, John. *Iran*. London, 1963.

Marek, J., and H. Knizkova. *The Jenghiz Khan Miniatures from the Court of Akbar the Great*. London, 1963.

Martens, Frederick H. "Mahomet and Music." *Musical Quarterly* (1926), 376–399.

Massoudieh, Mohammad Taghi. *Awaz-e Sur: Zur Melodiebildung in der persischen Kunstmusik*. Regensburg, 1968.

Mauguin, Bernard. "L'appel à la prière dans l'Islam." In *Encyclopédie des musiques sacrées*, ed. Jacques Porte. Paris, 1968. I, 404–408.

Melik-Aslanian, Emanuel. "By Way of Ecstasy." *Kahyan International* (Jan. 27, 1964), p. 6.

Merriam, Alan P. *The Anthropology of Music*. Evanston, 1964.

Meyer, Leonard B. *Music, the Arts, and Ideas*. Chicago, 1967.

Miller, Lloyd. *A Survey of Oriental Music*. East-West Records, n.d.

———, *A Survey of Oriental Music and Indo-Iranian Music and Its Influence*. East-West Records, n.d.

Mitjana, R. "L'orientalisme musical et la musique arabe." *Le monde oriental* 1 (1906), 184–222.

Mokri, Mohammad. "La musique sacrée des Kurdes *Fidèles de vérité*." In *Encyclopédie des musiques sacrées*, ed. Jacques Porte. Paris, 1968. I, 441–453.

———, "Le Soufisme et la musique." In *Encyclopédie de la musique*. Paris, 1961. III, 1014–1015.

"Music." *Iran Almanac 1961*, pp. 708–715. Tehran, 1961.

Nasr, Hossein. *Three Muslim Sages*. Cambridge, Mass., 1964.

Nettl, Bruno. "Examples of Folk and Popular Music from Khorasan." In *Festschrift für Walter Graf*. Forthcoming.

———, "Attitudes toward Persian Music in Tehran." *Musical Quarterly* 56 (1970), 183–197.

———, *Daramad of Chahargah: A Study in the Performance Practice of Persian Music*. Detroit, 1972.

———, "Persian Popular Music in 1969," *Ethnomusicology* 16 (1972), 218–239.

———, *Theory and Method in Ethnomusicology*. New York, 1964.

Nicholson, Reynold A. "Mysticism." In *The Legacy of Islam*, ed. Thomas Arnold and Alfred Guillaume.

———, *Rumi: Poet and Mystic*. London, 1950.

———, *Studies in Islamic Mysticism*. London, 1941.

Ordoobadi, Ahmad. *The Sufi Journey*. London, 1960.

Picken, Laurence. Review of *Musical Anthology of the Orient*. *JIFMC* 14 (1962), 140–142.

Polin, Claire C. J. *Music of the Ancient Near East*. New York, 1954.

Pope, Arthur U. *A Brief Outline of Persian Art*. New York, 1945.

———, and Phyllis Ackerman, eds. *A Survey of Persian Art*. 6 vols. London, 1939.

Qureshi, Regula. "Tarannum: The Chanting of Urdu Poetry," *Ethnomusicology* 13 (1969), 425–468.

Ranking, G. S. *The Elements of Arabic and Persian Prosody*. Bombay, 1885.

Rawlinson, George. *Parthia*. London, 1893.

Reese, Gustav. *Music in the Middle Ages*. New York, 1940.

Reinhard, Kurt. *Türkische Musik*. Berlin, 1962.

———, "Types of Turkmenian Songs in Turkey." *JIFMC* 9 (1957), 49–54.

Rezvani, Medjid. *Le théâtre et la danse en Iran*. Paris, 1963.

Ribera, Julian. *La Música de las Cantigas*. Madrid, 1922. Trans. and abr. as *Music in Ancient Arabia and Spain* by Eleanor Hague and Marion Leffingwell. London and Stanford, 1929.

Rice, Cyprian. *The Persian Sufis*. London, 1964.

Rice, David T. *Islamic Art*. Thames and Hudson, 1965.

Ritter, Helmut. "Der Reigen der 'Tanzenden Derwische.'" *Zeitschrift für vergleichende Musikwissenschaft* 1 (1933), ii.

Robson, James. *Ancient Arabian Instruments*. Glasgow, 1938.

———, "Kitab al-Malahi of Abu Talib al-Mufad al ibn Salama." Trans., with notes and introduction by Henry G. Farmer. *JRAS* (1938), 231–249.

———, "A Maghribi MS. on Listening to Music." *Islamic Culture* 27 (1952), 113–131.

Ronzevalle, L. "Un traité de musique arabe moderne." *Mélanges de la faculté orientale de l'Université St. Joseph de Beyrouth* 6 (1913), 1–120.

Rouanet, Jules. "La musique arabe," "La musique arabe dans le maghreb." In *Encyclopédie de la musique*, ed. Albert Lavignac and Lionel de la Laurencie. Paris, 1922.

Rousseau, Jean Jacques. *Dictionnaire de la musique*. Paris, 1768. (Chanson Persane, planche N).

Roychoudhury, M. L. "Music in Islam." *Journal of the Royal Asiatic Society* 23 (1957), 47–102.

Sachs, Curt. *The History of Musical Instruments*. New York, 1940.

———, *Real-Lexikon der Musikinstrumente*. Berlin, 1913; New York, 1963.

———, *The Rise of Music in the Ancient World*. New York, 1943.

———, *The Wellsprings of Music*. The Hague, 1962.

Sain, Kanwar. "An Old Manuscript on Iranian Music." *Indo-Iranica* 8 (1955), 29–36.

Saygun, Adnan. "Musique turque." In *L'histoire de la musique*, ed. Roland Manuel. *Encyclopédie de la Pléiade*, vol. 9. Paris.

Schmidt, Erich F. *Excavations at Tepe Hissar*. Philadelphia, 1937.

Schneider, Marius. "Maqam," "Nomos," "Raga." In *Die Musik in Geschichte und Gegenwart*, ed. Fredrich Blume. Kassel, 1962.

Schlesinger, Kathleen. *Is European Musical Theory Indebted to the Arabs?* London, 1925.

Seven Thousand Years of Iranian Art. Smithsonian Institute Publication No. 4543. Washington, D.C., 1964.

Sherley, Anthony. *Sir Anthony Sherley and His Persian Adventure*, ed. E. Denison Ross. London, 1933.

Shiloah, Amnon. *Caracteristiques de l'art vocal arabe au moyan-age*. Tel Aviv, 1963.

———, "Deux testes arabes inedits sur la musique." *Yuval*, Studies of the Jewish Music Research Centre. Jerusalem, 1968.

———, "L'epitre sur la musique des Ikhwan al-Safa, traduction annotée," *Revue des études islamiques* (1966).

———, "L'Islam et la musique." In *Encyclopédie des musiques sacrées*, ed. Jacques Porte. Paris, 1968.

Shirvastava, S. K. "Rag-Darpan (Music during the Mughal Period)." *Indian Historical Congressional Proceedings* 16 (1953), 256–267.

Sirajul, H. "Sama^c and Raqs of the Darwishes." *Islamic Culture* 18 (1944), 111–130.

Soheil, Afnan, M. *Avicenna: His Life and Works*. London, 1958.

Spector, Johanna. "Classical ʾUd Music in Egypt with Special Reference to *Maqamat*," *Ethnomusicology* 14 (1970), 243–257.

———, "Musical Tradition and Innovation." In *Central Asia: A Century of Russian Rule*, ed. Edward Allworth. New York, 1967.

———, "Special Bibliography." *Ethnomusicology* 3 (1959), 18–22. [Articles and reviews on folk and art music of the Central Asiatic peoples from *Sovietskaya Musika*, 1950–1955.]

Stafford, William. "The Music of the Persians and Turks." *American Art Journal* 33 (May 1, 1880), 4; (May 29, 1880), 65.

Sykes, Percy. *A History of Persia*. 2 vols. London, 1930.

———, "Notes on Musical Instruments in Khorasan, with Special Reference to the Gypsies." *Man* 9 (1909), 161–164.

Szabolcsi, Bence. *A History of Melody.* London, 1965.

Tagore, S. M., ed. *Hindu Music from Various Authors.* Calcutta, 1875.

Thevenot. *The Travels of Monsieur de Thevenot into the Levant.* London, 1687.

Touma, Habib H. "Maqam: A Form of Improvisation." In *The World of Music* 12 (1970), 22–31.

———, "The Maqam Phenomenon: An Improvisation Technique in the Music of the Middle East." *Ethnomusicology* 15 (January 1971), 38–48.

Tsuge, Gen²ichi. "Music of Persia." Unpublished course outline. Wesleyan University, February–May 1967.

———, Review of recording *Classical Music of Iran. Ethnomusicology* 15 (January 1971), 152–154.

———, "Rhythmic Aspects of the *Avaz* in Persian Music." *Ethnomusicology* 14 (1970), 205–227.

Vandenberghe, L. "Les Reliefs élamites de Malamir." *Iranica antiqua* 3 (1963).

Virolleaud, Charles. *Le théâtre persan ou le drame de Kerbela.* Paris, 1950.

Webb, F. G. Discussion of Henry G. Farmer's "The Influence of Music from Arabic Sources." *Proceedings of the Musical Association* 52–53 (April 27, 1926).

Weil, Gotthold. "Arud." In *Encyclopedia of Islam.* Leiden, 1936.

Wellesz, Egon. "Probleme der musikalischen Orientforschung." *Peters Jahrbuch* 24 (1917), 2–18.

Werner, Eric. "Greek Ideas in Music in Judeo-Arabic Literature." In *The Commonwealth of Music*: Essays in Honor of Curt Sachs, ed. Gustav Reese and Rose Brandel, pp. 71–96. New York, 1965.

———, and Isaiah Sonne. "The Philosophy and Theory of Music in Judao-Arabic Literature." *Hebrew Union College Annual* 16 (1941), 251–319; 17 (1942–43), 511–575.

Wilber, Donald. *Iran, Past and Present.* Princeton, 1958.

———, "Persian Village Songs." *Bulletin of the Iranian Institute of America* (1946), 151–157.

Wilkens, Eckart. *Künstler und Amateure im persischen Santurspiel.* Studien zum Gestaltungsvermögen in der iranischen Musik. Kölner Beiträge zur Musikforschung, vol. 45. Regensburg, 1967.

Wright, Owen. "Ibn al-Munajjim and the Early Arabian Modes." *The Galpin Society Journal* 19 (1966), 27–48.

Yekta Bey, Raouf. "La musique turque." In *Encyclopédia de la musique.* ed. Albert Lavignac and Lionel de la Laurencie. Paris, 1922.

Zonis, Ella. "Classical Persian Music Today." In *Iran Faces the Seventies*, ed. Ehsan Yar-Shater. New York, 1971.

———, "Contemporary Art Music in Persia." *Musical Quarterly* 51 (1965), 636–648. Repr. as The University of Chicago, Center for Middle Eastern Studies, Reprint Series, No. 2.

———, "Improvisation in Persian Music." In *Improvisation in Music: East and West*, ed. Ella Zonis and Leonard B. Meyer. Chicago, forthcoming.

————, "Persia." In *Harvard Dictionary of Music*, 2d. ed., by Willi Apel.

————, "Radife Moussighiye Iran." *Ethnomusicology* 8 (1964), 303–310.

————, Review of *Daramad of Chahargah: A Study in the Performance Practice of Persian Music*. *Asian Music Journal*, forthcoming.

————, Review of recording: *Kurdish Folk Music From Western Iran*, Folkways FE 4103. *Ethnomusicology* 13 (1969), 204–205.

————, Review of *Musikgeschichte in Bildern: Islam*. *Journal of the American Musicological Society* 22 (1969), 293–296.

BOOKS AND ARTICLES IN PERSIAN OR ARABIC

An asterisk denotes musical score.

Al-Rajab, Hashim Muhammad. *Al Maqam al Iraqi*. Baghdad, 1961.

Aref (Ghazvini). *Divan*. Tehran, 1327 (1948).

Badi^c va ^cAruz Qafieh. Tehran, 1343 (1964).

Baharlu, Mohammad. **Ketab-e Sevom-e Musiqi-ye Iran*. Tehran, 1336 (1957).

————, **Ketab-e Chaharom-e Musiqi-ye Iran*. Tehran, 1337 (1958).

Forugh, Mehdi. "Talfiq-e Sheir va Musiqi." *Majaleh-ye Musiqi* 17–32 (1336–1337 [1957–58]).

Hedayat, Mehdi Gholi. *Madjma^cal Advar*. Tehran, 1317 (1938).

————, ***"Radif-e Musiqi-ye Iran." Tehran, 1337 qamari (1915).

Jahed, Amir. **Divan*. Tehran, 1305 (1926). Musical score and articles.

Khaleqi, Ruhollah. **Dastur-e Moqadamati, Tar va Sehtar*. Tehran, 1330 (1951), Jeld-e dovom, Tehran, 1331 (1952).

————, *Ham Ahangi Musiqi*. Tehran, 1320 (1941).

————, *Majaleh-ye Chang*. Tehran, 1325 (1946).

————, "Modulation dar Musiqi-ye Irani." *Majaleh-ye Musiqi* 60–61 (1340 [1961]).

————, *Musiqi-ye Iran*. Tehran, 1342 (1963).

————, *Nazari be Musiqi*. 2 vols. Tehran, 1316, 1317 (1937, 1938).

————, *Sargozasht-e Musiqi-ye Iran*. 3 vols. I, Tehran, 1333 (1954); II, Tehran, 1334 (1955); III, in *Musik-e Iran* 89–97 (1338–1339 [1959–1960]).

————, **Violin: Ketab-e Aval, Dovom, Sevom, Chaharom*. Tehran, 1330, 1331, 1332, 1334 (1951, 1952, 1953, 1955).

Khalkhali, Sayed Abad al Rahim. *Divan Hafez-e Shirazi*. Tehran, 1306 (1927).

Khanlari, Parviz Natal. *Vazn-e Sheir-e Farsi*. Tehran, 1337 (1958).

Ma^cruffi, Mussa. **Avaz-e Dashti, Daftar-e Aval*. Tehran, 1327 (1948).

————, **Avaz-e Chahargah*. Tehran, n.d.

————, ***"Radif-e Musiqi-ye Iran." In *La musique traditionelle de l'Iran*. Tehran, 1963.

Mahmudi, Manucher, **Shish Ahang-e Mahali*. Tehran, 1328 (1949).

Majaleh-ye Musiqi. Jeld-e Sevom, Zavin Hacobian, ed. Tehran, 1956 ff.

Majaleh-ye Musiqi-ye Radio Iran. Tehran, 1957 ff.

Mallah, Hossein. "Tasnif Chist?" *Majaleh-ye Musiqi* 13 and 14 (1336 [1957]).

Manucheri (Domghani). *Divan.* Ed. Mohammad Dabirsiᶜaghi. Tehran, 1326 (1947).

Mirabadini, Abutalleb. *Lalaᶜi.* Tehran, 1337 (1958).

Mobassheri, Lutfollah. *Ahang-haye Mahali.* Tehran, 1338 (1959).

Muzik-e Iran. Ed. E. Bahman Hirbod. Tehran, 1952 ff.

Nasir (Mira Nasir Forsat-e Dowleh). *Bohur el Alhan.* Tehran, 1332 (1953).

Payan, Lutfollah. ed. *Bist o Panj Qateh-ye Zarbi.* Tehran, 1327 (1948).

———, *Davazdah Tasnif as Davazdah Avaz.* Tehran, 1339 (1960).

———, *Hijdah Qateh-ye Pish-Daramad.* 3d ed. Tehran, 1335 (1956).

———, *Tarana Mahali.* Tehran, n.d.

Payan, Lutfollah Moqadam. *Gamha-ye Iran.* Tehran, 1335 (1956).

Payvar, Faramarz. *Dastur-e Santur.* Tehran, n.d.

Razani, Abu Tarab. *Sheir va Musiqi.* Tehran, 1340 (1961).

Saba, Abol Hassan. *Durey-e Aval-e Santur.* 2d ed. Tehran, 1337 (1958).

———, *Durey Dovom-e Santur.* Tehran, 1335 (1956).

———, *Durey-e Sevom-e Santur.* 2d ed. Tehran, 1337 (1958).

———, *Durey-e Chaharom-e Santur.* Tehran, 1339 (1960).

———, *Durey-e Aval-e Violin.* 4th ed. Tehran, 1339 (1960).

———, *Durey-e Dovom-e Violin.* 3d ed. Tehran, 1338 (1959).

———, *Durey-e Sevom-e Violin.* 2d ed. Tehran, 1337 (1958).

———, *Durey-e Aval-e Tar va Sehtar.* Tehran, 1339 (1960).

Saba, Hossein. *Khod Amuz Santur.* Tehran, 1343 (1964).

Sheybani, Aziz. *Tarana-haye Mahali-ye Azerbajan,* 4 vols. Tehran, 1333 (1954).

Tarmedi, Adib Sabar, *Avazn Sheir-e Arabi va Farsi,* ed. Mujtaba Minovi. Tehran, n.d.

Vaziri, Ali Naqi. *Dastur-e Tar.* Berlin, 1913; Tehran, 1315 (1936).

———, *Dastur-e Violin.* Tehran, 1312 (1933).

———, *Musiqi-ye Nazari.* Tehran, 1313 (1934).

———, *Sorud-haye Madares.* Tehran, 1312 (1933).

Zonis, Ella. "Radif-e musiqi-ye Iran." *Majaleh-ye Musiqi* 83 and 84, 1342 (1963).

MEDIEVAL ARABIC TREATISES

The treatises pertinent to this study are the following, which are numbered as they appear in Henry G. Farmer's bibliography *The Sources of Arabian Music* (Leiden, 1965).

Al-Kindi: 49, 53.

Arabic translations of Greek theorists: 85–113.

Al-Farabi: 159, 167.

Abu⁣ᶜl Faraj al-Isfahani: 175
Ikhwan al Safa: 192.
Ibn Sina: 202, 203
Ibn Zaila: 210.
Al-Ghazali: 218.
Safi al Din: 252, 253.
Al-Shirazi: 261.
Al-Amuli: 276 (in Persian).
Al-Qaramani (*Kanz al Tuhaf*): 277 (in Persian).
Al-Jurjani: 295.
Ibn Ghabi al Maraghi: 300 (in Persian).

Discography

Classical Music of Iran, Dastgah Systems. Compiled and edited by Ella Zonis. Folkways FW 8831, 8832.

Folk Songs and Dances of Iran. Notes written by Anthony Byan Shay. Folkways FW 8858.

Kurdish Folk Music from Western Iran. Recorded by Dieter and Nerthus Christensen, notes by Dieter Christensen, ed. by Frank Gillis. Ethic Folkways Library FE 4103.

The Middle East: Modes and Melodies of the Middle East. Lloyd Miller, East-West Records.

Music of Iran: Santur Recital. Nasser Rastegar-Najad. 3 vols. Lyrichord LL 135, 165, 166, LLST 7135, 7165, 7166.

Music of Iran, the Tar. Bijan Samandar. Lyrichord LL 201, LLST 7201.

Music of the Russian Middle East. Notes by Henry Cowell, Ethnic Folkways Library FE 4416.

A Musical Anthology of the Orient: Iran I and II. Recordings and commentaries by Alain Danielou. Barenreiter-Musicaphon, UNESCO Collection, BM 30 L 2004, 2005.

Near and Far East. Lloyd Miller. East-West Records.

Santur, Tunbuk, and Tar: Music and Drum Rhythms from Iran. Edited by Deben Bhattacharya. Limelight Stereo, LS 86057.

Index

229